Dancing
IN THE
UNKNOWN

Dancing
IN THE
UNKNOWN

Printed in the United States of America

First Printing, 2017

ISBN 978-0-692-90415-2

betsychasse.net/dancing-in-the-unknown/

Edited by: Debbie Spector Weisman
Cover and book design by Jill Hawkins

Dancing IN THE UNKNOWN

Betsy Chasse

Betsy Chasse is an award-winning filmmaker including *What The Bleep Do We Know?!* and *Song of The New Earth*, and the author of five books including *Tipping Sacred Cows* and *It Came Out Of My Vagina, Now What?* She recently completed production on a short documentary, *The Empty Womb*, which explores one woman's journey through infertility and how art helped her to heal and *Radical Dating*, a web series which follows five singles over forty as they embark on a journey to find lasting love.

She is a Mom of two, Elora, thirteen, and Max, ten. Since their births they have shown Betsy how to Dance in The Unknown and together they enjoy all sorts of wild adventures.

Preface

"The only way to make sense out of change is to plunge into it, move with it and join the dance."
–ALAN W. WATTS

ARE YOU READY TO DANCE IN THE UNKNOWN?

Knowledge is Safe. *RIGHT?* To know means we're grounded, we've got this. Or does it? Is it possible that *"knowing"* is our silent soul killer? Is knowledge the key that has locked us into the darkest of dungeons? Is knowing what to do or what we should do always what our soul wants?

What? I thought knowledge was a good thing. When I say Knowledge, I don't mean as in the knowing of facts, as in 1+1=2. That's indisputable…even in our age of "alternative facts". I mean, what "I" know.

One night under the stars as I contemplated my life, its meaning and purpose and the why's about why I am where I am and doing what I'm doing, the word *Knowledge* danced around in my head. I noticed that there are two words in that one big word:

KNOW and LEDGE…

Let that sink in….

KNOW and LEDGE...

Huh... interesting.
I put the words together like this. The more I *"know"*, the closer to the *"ledge"* I am.
What ledge? Is this a good thing or a bad thing? Ledges can go either way.
How do we *"know"?*

We know by experience; our past, the moments we've lived, have shaped what we *know*. Our ability to *know what we know* has been shaped by such input as education, parenting, current affairs, selfies and cell phones. Our entire world view is made up from our past and we love that. We love to *know* our story.

Sometimes this is a good thing, as in *"let's not step in that cesspool again, that was nasty"* and sometimes it's because there was a feeling of safety in *"knowing"*. Even if that safety was tainted with trauma and coping mechanisms, we made it safe. Safe is subjective, as in safe is what we feel when we *"know"*.

Ironically, the safety of knowing has made us prisoners of it. After all, the notion of questioning our own institutions, stories and beliefs is frightening. The hanging around in the question of...

WHAT IF?

is so ugly, dark and uncomfortable, that we'd rather to stay in the suffering we *"know"*.
However...

What happens if we jump off the ledge?
What happens if we ask **WHAT IF?**

Join me and men and women from all walks of life who said, "What if". These courageous people faced sickness, death, divorce, and much of life's traumas and chose to let go of their story, take a leap of faith and dance.

The stories in this book are from real people who've asked, **"What is knowledge? What if I didn't know"**, and stayed with it long enough to have a new experience, build new neuro-pathways, institutions and Sacred Cows which came from a deeper, more meaningful place. This journey impacted them so deeply that they cannot return to the "Known". Now they must Dance in the Unknown because they know this is where life happens.

That night as I sat under the stars, I thought about the world and the fear, hurt, anger and resentment festering deep and in many ways exploding outward into the streets. I was saddened that many of us aren't living the lives our soul craved. I'm sure many are probably not even sure what they want or how to achieve it. No wonder the world is seemingly imploding. The soul can suffer for a long time, and yet eventually its great desire for the light will force it to do anything to feel its glow-anything. This is when a crisis usually shows up, often out of nowhere – or so we think.

Everyone in this book has had that moment when their soul cried out to them and they chose to listen to it, to give it light.

I have had many of those moments which I have shared in other books and films. I decided that instead of me yammering on and on with stories I've already told, I'd invite others to share their stories.

Cate Montana

Cate Montana is the author of *The E Word: Ego, Enlightenment & Other Essentials* and *Unearthing Venus: My Search for the Woman Within*. Cate is a dauntless explorer of inner and outer worlds, has a master's degree in humanistic psychology and writes and teaches about the ego, transpersonal and transcendent consciousness, personal evolution and... wait for it... play. The former editor of *The Bleeping Herald* newsletter for the film *What the Bleep Do We Know!?* she currently writes for Lynne McTaggart's global alternative health magazine *What Doctors Don't Tell You* magazine (UK) and blogs for *The Huffington Post*.

Introduction

THE EGO AND THE UNKNOWN

By Cate Montana

Ever noticed how easy it is to fall into a habit pattern with the simplest of things, like putting on your left boot first, driving the same route to the store every time and saying "fine" when somebody asks how you are – whether you're fine or not?

I remember when it fully hit me how habitual I was. I was speaking at a conference in California and discovered that after only one trip to the Ladies Room, I automatically started heading to the same stall every time afterwards. Now that's habituation in action!

Bottom line, big issues or small, we love the comfort and convenience of the known. We don't have to think. We don't have to consciously choose what to say or do or where to go. We just follow the neurological pattern stamped in our brain – the familiar geography, the familiar sounds and smells, the familiar information – and presto! There we are, back in the same lane on the Interstate, driving the same car to the same job, eating the same thing on Wednesdays, using the same second-from-the-left stall with the squeaky hinges and the "Beware! Limbo Dancer Entry" graffiti with its downward-pointing arrow in the bathroom.

This is just the day-to-day physical navigation stuff!

Not only do we get into physical ruts, our entire identity – what is commonly called the ego – is created using the exact same dynamic. Seriously! Repeated sensory input (physical experience) = hard-wired neuron patterns in the brain = "you" and "me" and every other Joe and Josephine on the planet.

I know this doesn't sound very glamorous (and don't you know the ego loves to feel glamorous). I know the ego has a pretty bad reputation nowadays. How not? The egos on parade in politics and corporate America offer up a pretty ugly picture of what it means to have one. In religious and spiritual circles, the ego is basically regarded as the enemy. It's something we have to dissolve or banish, kill or subdue. But here's the thing: the ego is unkillable.

Why? Because as long as there is an individual witnessing consciousness connected to a physical body trying to dissolve itself, there will always be a continuing sense of self trying to complete the action... which perpetuates the ego.

Sorry! But take heart. Contrary to popular belief, this is not a bad thing at all.

The ego is simply who we think we are. It's the sense of individual self that enables us to have the wonderful experience of living in a physical body. It's a tool that allows us to function on planet Earth – the structure that allows us to interact and distinguish "self" from "other". And don't you know, if the "other" is a school bus barreling down the road toward you at forty-five miles per hour, being able to know where "you" are in space/time in relation to the bus' position in space/time is a good thing!

The ego is inevitable, infinitely practical and ultimatly a gift. The only time it becomes problematic is when human beings don't know what the ego is, what it's for, how to manage it or who they really are deep down beneath the ego's sensory program. Which is, of course, why the world is in the shape it's in today.

We don't know or do any of that.

THE EGO AND THE UNKNOWN

The trick about the ego is learning to manage the gift. How BIG can my sense of self become?

When I talk about big, I'm not talking about ego inflation, as in "Boy, does he ever have a swelled head." I'm talking about big as in, "How much life can I contain?" How great can I become?" How inclusive can I be? How much wisdom can I gain and express about life? How much beauty can I shine into dark places? How much love can I feel and give? How much of the unknown can I make known in this lifetime?

That's BIG.

But to get to the place of bigness – to be able to expand beyond our habits, both physical and mental, and move into the vast unknown territory that is the rest of "you" and "me" – the first and foremost thing to understand is what the ego is (our sense of personal self) and how the ego is born out of our body's senses. Once we truly grasp the physical root of identity, then we can understand and let go of the fears and doubts that keep us small, habitual and selfish, and begin to shine!

HOW THE EGO IS BORN

For months after our birth, we swim in a bath of sensory information. It's a wild time! Undifferentiated sights and sounds and smells and touches flood our baby brains with eleven million bits of sensory data every second and we don't know what to make of it at first. It's a tsunami! But slowly our brains learn to pick out patterns. We begin to see "mommy" as different from "the wall". We don't have words for "mommy" and "wall" yet. But all the same we see and feel and smell and taste the difference.

We also quickly learn that mommy, daddy, the wall, the milk bottle and the dog are different from "me". The body tells us where "I" leave off in space/time and where "mommy" begins – or the teddy bear and blanket. Our brains quickly learn what is "self" and "other than self." Then, as soon as we begin to learn language, we are given words to describe this sense of self and "other". We learn a sound and learn it is our name. We learn pronouns, "he" and "she" and "you" and "us" and "them".

Without ever being aware of it, we learn we are separate from everything and everyone else in existence. This unconscious sense of separation is where the root of all our fear starts and our problems with the ego begin.

The deeper truth of the matter is, we are not separate and we aren't alone at all.

Mystics from Buddha to Jesus have taught that humans are part of the indivisible One – that the nature of reality is wholeness and inclusion, not distance and apartness. Starting in the early 20th century, quantum physicists from Einstein to Schrödinger to Stephen Hawking came to the same conclusions. Peering through electron microscopes and smashing atoms together in vast particle accelerators, scientists have not been able to find any borders, boundaries or walls between different, apparently separate, "things" at all!

Where our material eyes see distance and differences, boundaries and separation, the eyes of spirit and science see only an undifferentiated dance of energy where every "thing" is one with every other "thing" in existence and part of the Whole.

Unfortunately, this is not the reality we humans live in. Until, that is, we begin to learn the truth about our selves – that we are actually formless spirit/consciousness: and the truth about the world – that it is part of us and nothing to be afraid of. Once we begin to wrap our heads around that, we begin the interesting journey of understanding the ego – our ideas about who we are as we live out the illusion our bodies give us that we're isolated stand-alone units called human beings.

Can you imagine how safe you'd feel if you knew you were one with all life? How comforted you'd feel knowing you were intimately joined in an eternal dance with everyone around you? How kind and compassionate you'd be if you grasped the truth that everyone around you actually was you at the most fundamental level of existence?

Wow! Who would there be to compete with? Who would you fear? Who would be above you? Or below?

No one.

This is a book about dancing into the unknown. As (apparently) physical beings, we have a tendency to think about the unknown in terms of space exploration and mysterious aliens,

ancient civilizations and the Akashic Records, secret rites of Tibetan lamas, alternate dimensions and astral travel… all of which sound very exciting and enticing.

But the truth is, the unknown also includes such things as peace, harmony, deep fulfillment, joy for no reason, love, ecstasy, bliss and all those other wonderful states of being that we yearn for but only taste occasionally. We have no idea what it would be like to experience these states as our natural way of being – it's a complete unknown. The only way we can enter into that ecstatic place is by diving full on into the biggest unknown of all – our true selves.

THE GATEWAY

The gateway to the true self lies in identifying who we think we are, and then realizing that who we really are is everything else but those things that we believe ourselves to be!

I am a physical human being, I am a man, I am a woman, I am a teacher, I am a social worker, a writer, a contractor, a bus driver – a tall black bus driver, a short Jewish waitress, a poor starving artist, a tofu-eating spiritual bookkeeper. Sorry! Not! Those things are not who we are. They're what our bodies look like. They're what we do for a living. They're conditions we live in and beliefs we hold. But what about the true self that underlies and supports all this doing, having and believing?

That is a complete unknown.

The good news is that, despite popular spiritual beliefs to the contrary – despite the programming we all absorb as we grow up that says the path to truth is hard and arduous – it doesn't have to be that way. Unless, that is, we want it to be! The ego loves complexity. It thrives upon systems and beliefs. Its whole existence depends upon how complicated and tough it can make things. But who is making the journey hard?

Your ego – the person you think you are but are not.

It's actually quite simple to tap into who you really are. Here's a little exercise that shows you just how simple!

Make a list of all the things you think you are. Start each statement with the words I AM. Here's my list to give you an example:

I am a human being
I am a woman
I am Caucasian
I am smart
I am a writer
I am a socialist
I am an athlete
I am a resident of the world
I am a lover of life
I am a playshop leader
I am a public speaker
I am a gardener
I am a hiker
I am a swimmer
etc.

Write out your list, then read that list out loud. Notice how each statement makes you feel. Sense the energy behind the words as you declare to the universe who and what you are. If it helps, close your eyes as you make each statement. Run through the whole list again – out loud. Sense the energy

qualifying the words I AM.

But this time when you get to the end of your statements say aloud:

I AM

Be quiet for a few moments. Sense the difference. Feel the empty spaciousness when you simply say I AM and don't follow it with anything.

The empty spaciousness is who you really are.

Play with this. Your ego might say it's too simple – too easy – too silly. But hey. What sounds less habitual, more exciting, fun and free and filled with the unknown:

I am complicated

or

I AM …

The choice is yours!

Debbie Spector Weisman

Debbie Spector Weisman has incorporated the knowledge gleaned from her professional work and as a wife and mother into Dream-Life Coaching. In addition to her coaching work, Debbie has been the co-owner of a film and video production company which was instrumental in the production of dozens of films including the groundbreaking film *What the Bleep Do We Know!?*, *Man of the Year*, starring John Ritter, *Pregnant in America*, and the spiritual documentary *Dreaming Heaven*. Debbie is also the best-selling author of over twenty novels, including five of the original books in the popular *Sweet Valley High* series. She credits her dream work with inspiring her to return to writing. Her most recent books include *101 Dream Dates: How to Say I Love You To the Most Important Person in Your Life--You!* and the best-seller *It Came Out of My Vagina, Now What?!*, co-written with Betsy Chasse. She is also featured in the books *Chicken Soup For The Soul: Dreams and Premonitions, Recipes for Living, Vols 1 and 3, My Creative Thoughts, Ask Coach* and *Dreams That Change Our Lives*. Debbie is a member of the International Association for the Advancement of Dreams and the Holistic Chamber of Commerce. For more, go to thedreamcoach.net

Chapter One

ENLIGHTENED YOLO

By Debbie Spector Weisman

"...you never see further than your headlights, but you can make the whole trip that way."
—E.L. Doctorow

Recently my husband and I were waiting in line for the ferry from Bridgeport, Connecticut, to Port Jefferson, New York. Being in the front row of cars waiting to enter, we had a bird's eye view of the drivers leaving the arriving ferry. To pass the time, we decided to play a game: That guy looks happy; that one's grouchy; that one can't wait to get off the boat; that one looks distracted; that one looks like he's never been happy his entire life.

Then it was our turn to drive on to the ship. It being a beautiful summer day, I decided to walk to the front railing and spend the trip gazing out at the glorious view. I couldn't have asked for a more picture-perfect day. A light gentle breeze kept the temperature at a delightfully refreshing 77 degrees. The view went on forever. I could see sailboats miles in the distance gently rolling on the waves. I was nearly mesmerized by the gentle ebb and flow of the water below me. I was marveling at how this easy, enjoyable ride was such a creative and stress-relieving alternative from the bumper to bumper traffic we would have endured snaking around the outskirts of New York City and into the far reaches of Long Island to get to our destination. I raised my face to the sun and gave silent thanks for having the opportunity to enjoy this lovely boat ride.

Then I thought back to those people who had gotten off the ferry. They had experienced the same excursion and a good deal of them came off the boat, scowling. Why? You couldn't have asked for more perfect conditions for this ride. Why hadn't their spirits been uplifted from this joy-inducing experience?

I didn't have to look far to get the answer. There was a time I'd probably not have appreciated the trip too. My mind would have been focused on how expensive it was, how the wind was messing up my hair, how I was exposing myself to cancer-enduring sun rays or even some other totally unrelated thought that would have clouded my mind from the wonderful experience that was happening right before my eyes.

I had changed my mindset. I had come to realize something simple and profound. You only live once – YOLO. We all know that and know how we should all strive to enjoy every moment and live the best lives possible. Yet most of us fall short – good god, I know I had for a good part of my life.

I must admit I've spent years agonizing over the small stuff and have even thrown myself into depression over things that were never in my control and, in the end, not worth the psychic price it paid in my soul. I did all the conventional things that people in those circumstances do. I sought out therapy – lots of it. I popped a lot of the pills that were supposed to make me happy, from Prozac to Paxil to Wellbutrin. They did the trick for a while but I always chose to get off those meds because deep down I knew they weren't the answer. Not to mention that

Paxil made me gain weight I didn't want which added to my depression and seemed so counterproductive. I also didn't like the idea of taking all those chemicals and switched to the more natural St. John's Wort for a while. That didn't make a difference and I stopped that too.

I remember sitting through therapy sessions when I'd be asked to pour out my agonies and I could do a great job describing whatever was the latest slight I felt life had thrown at me. Each of the therapists I saw were kind and attentive and really believed they were there to help. I'd leave the sessions feeling a bit better and would quit when I felt I was "cured". Then something would happen that would trigger a relapse and I'd go through the same roller coaster of emotions, usually ending up feeling okay yet always having an unsure feeling that any happiness was fleeting and I was doomed to live through crisis after crisis, leaving me to grab those moments of elation when I could because I knew they could go away as quickly as they came.

What I've come to realize now is that in all those years of therapy and pill popping, I never was forced to deal with the real root of my discontent: my lack of self-love. I had all those voices in my head telling me over and over that I was worthless, that I was unlovable and didn't deserve to have happiness. Boy, did those voices hate me. With all that noise swirling around in my brain, no wonder I had days when I had to wonder why I was bothering to hang around.

Yet here I am, writing to you now to say that life is beautiful and rich and that I am a wonderful being with lots of love for myself and even more to share with others.

What turned me around? Conch fritters.

It may sound silly or even unbelievable that one meal could in-still deep self-love within me. Truthfully, perhaps it wasn't just this one meal, but it is symbolic of the transformation that arose within me. Here's what happened.

I was in Florida visiting my mother, who, at the time, was in the hospital. One night she urged me to go out and get some-thing to eat. (Let's face it, once a Jewish mother, always a Jewish mother concerned that – God forbid--her child, even her capable adult child, not starve to death.) Till then, going out meant a trip down to the cafeteria or some fast food takeout on the way back to her condo. The thought of going to a restaurant by myself was, now that I look back on it, frightening. I'd feel self-conscious, convinced that all eyes would be staring at the lonely looking woman sitting by herself at night. It didn't mat-ter to me what any of those people were thinking. Just the idea of their being people seeing me eat alone was enough to deter me from seeking something more satisfying than drive-thru Chicken McNuggets.

On that trip, something had changed. Not too long before that, I had discovered dreamwork and was in my training to become a Dream-Life Coach. Working with my dreams had taught me a lot about how much I could learn though my subconscious thoughts which manifested themselves in my dreams. You see, when we go to sleep, the conscious part of our brain that runs our lives during the day turns off. The limbic part of our brain, the part that holds our subconscious and our visual cortex wakes up. This is where dreaming takes place and all those images and thoughts that emerge when we dream are unfiltered and pure. What that means is that they're not bogged down by the chatter we hear in our minds during the day, all those thou-sands and thousands of words – mostly negative – that tend to instill not very productive beliefs like I'm not good enough, I'm ugly, I'm unlovable, I'm a failure, etc.

By learning how to pay attention to my dreams, I had come to realize that I had been listening to all that awful chatter – and believing it! I'd be lying if I said I had an overnight transformation – I didn't – but gradually I had retrained my thick skull into believing a different understanding about myself. Why would I say I wasn't good enough or that I was a failure? I had a loving husband, had raised two children into productive adulthood, been a best-selling author who'd sold millions of books, co-ran a Hollywood production company and even co-produced a couple of movies. A neutral observer might call that being a success, yet my own mind – the one that really matters – thought otherwise for a very long time. Why would I think I was ugly? I was never very happy about my being short but I'd had others complement me on my "petite" figure and I was proud to have kept my weight stable for years. When I was a kid I hated my curly hair but in my adult years I loved being able to style it by running my fingers though it and not being a slave to a blow dryer.

Yet my mind had thought otherwise. None of that had mattered when I chose to listen to my self-induced lies or had inflated my stumbles into events that dwarfed all my achievements. It was that negative thinking that had led me to fall into depression. When I was in those dark moods all I could hear was the negative self-talk. It was crazy but true. I could think two thoughts about myself – one good, one bad – and the negative one would win out every time. There was nothing wrong with me except what I was telling myself was wrong about me.

When I could see that my mind chatter was false, life took a turn for the positive. The key was the awareness. When I could see I was letting a dark thought cloud over me, I was able to

stop it in its tracks. Often it was something as simple as cor-
recting myself when I'd say, "I'm stupid" when spilling coffee
over my morning newspaper. In the past, I'd believe that. In
this new state of awareness, however, I could correct myself and
rephrase the incident simply as "I spilled the coffee". That was a
true statement of fact but without the judgment attached.

Multiply that event with the thousands of little missteps I'd
make from time to time and you can see how that could make a
difference in my self-perception.

Old habits die hard, though, and when it came to going out to
dinner that night in Florida, my first thought was to pick up
some take out and eat alone in the relative comfort of my mother's condo. Then a more enlightened thought came up. One of
my favorite foods I liked to eat when visiting my mother was a
local delicacy, conch fritters. I knew of a restaurant right on the
beach that served them. What was stopping me from going there?

I could make a case that a lot was stopping me. I would be
by myself. There might be a crowd and that would make me
uncomfortable. The server might look at me strangely or make
a judgment about me.

Take a look at that last paragraph. Is there anything there that
looks like a fact? Anything there that is a real, legitimate reason
for staying away from the restaurant? Let me answer that question for you: No. That was my old mind finding reasons to keep
me from doing something my heart wanted to do. My mind was
focusing on the negative, even straining to come up with excuses
that wanted to make sense and only made sense if I chose to believe them unquestionably. Once I held those thoughts up to the
light of day, even my stubborn mind could see that they made
no sense. *This is my life to lead*, I thought. You only live once.

Why deny yourself something that's so easy to satisfy?

That was all I needed to get into the car and go to the restaurant. In a funny way, this venture would also satisfy one of the class requirements for my training program. Each student was required to go on a "Dream Date" once a week. This meant that we were to choose an activity that we would not normally do, something fun or possibly challenging, and do it by ourselves. The idea was that by spending this time with ourselves we'd gain a greater self-understanding, self-acceptance and, ultimately, greater self-love.

Up until then, I'd been resisting this part of the program. I'd considered myself a loner most of my life and that hadn't made me love myself very much. I didn't see how making a special effort to do something by myself was going to change that. But here I was being given a giant opportunity to take myself on a date. Might as well take the plunge. I got into the car and headed toward the beach.

It was early in the evening and the restaurant was not very crowded when I got there. Quickly I was led to a booth and given a menu. *Oh, no!* I gasped to myself as I scanned the food choices. *No conch fritters!* It didn't make sense to me as I had ordered them from this very same restaurant a year earlier. Yelp said they made some of the best conch fritters in the area. What was up with this?

In the past, I would have kept my disappointment to myself and settled for something else. I would have told myself some stupid reasoning, like I didn't deserve to get what I wanted or I was being punished for some unknown – but to my mind – very real reason. On that night, however, filled with the commitment to do something positive for myself, I did something I usually didn't do. I spoke up to the server and asked why the conch fritters weren't on the menu.

The server smiled at me. "Here they are." She pointed a finger at a line that somehow had escaped my vision.

At that point, I could have berated my mind again and called myself stupid for somehow having missed this obvious item. But I didn't. I acknowledged to myself that I missed it – again, statement of fact with no judgment attached – and let it go.

"Great," I said, realizing I was letting a smile cross my face as well. "While we're at it, I'd like a Cadillac Margarita as well."

Okay, perhaps not the healthiest meal for a great self-revelation. But that doesn't matter. My mother was ill and I was feeling the stress of what that meant. I deserved a night out and to indulge myself in something that would give me pleasure.

That was the revelation. I deserved to be happy. I was blessed to be given a life to live and I deserved to add happiness to that life. If even something as simple as a conch fritter could make me happy, I shouldn't be the one to stop myself from having it. I had a car to get there, I had legs to walk me to my seat, I had an appetite that demanded to be satisfied. I had life and was here to fulfill my wishes.

While I waited for the meal to arrive, I looked around me. The restaurant was on a pedestrian path adjacent to the beach. From where I sat I could look out beyond the sand to the beautiful turquoise ocean. Having grown up in a beach town, I always loved gazing at the ocean and I was thankful I had the opportunity to do this. I also enjoyed people-watching the steady stream that walked past the restaurant and gazed at the gulls that swooped down to pick at the crumbs left by earlier sunbathers. Behind me was the enjoyable sound of old rock hits emanating from the bar's sound system.

It didn't matter that I was sitting by myself. No one cared. Even more importantly, I didn't care. I was enjoying myself and that was all that mattered. The fritters were as tasty as I remembered them to be and the drink was equally satisfying.

"If this is what a Dream Date is about, why am I fighting it?" I asked myself. I felt my resistance crumble. Over the course of the next few months I went on more dates with myself, each one a little more creative than the next and over time a miracle happened. I really did fall in love with myself again.

Something magical happens when we embrace self-love. I'm not talking about the sexual kind, though that's important too. To me self-love starts with self-acceptance. It's the understanding that I am who I am, and who I am is perfect. That doesn't mean I don't have flaws or don't make mistakes. I do, just as we all do. But those things don't define me, diminish me or make me "less than". They're just fragments of the thousands of things that make me, me.

When I am aware of who I am, I can make the choice of what I do, where I go, who I want to be. I can choose to focus on my deficits or my mistakes and go into that self-defeating spiral I used to ride which often led to those depressive episodes. Or I can see those failures for what they are – momentary setbacks – and choose to learn from them and, hopefully, not make those mistakes again.

The more I began to love myself unconditionally, the more I felt my confidence grow. I took chances in areas I never explored.

I started a new business and revived a writing career that had stalled twenty years earlier. I saw the unknown as a place not to be feared but as a place of curiosity. I'll admit I didn't take a giant leap – it was more like baby steps – but even small steady steps will lead to miles of new discovery if taken with purpose, passion and desire. After all, you only live once. Why not make the most of every day?

The quote at the top of this piece was originally written about writing. I think it's apropos to this conversation as well. We are all on the road of life and don't always know where we're going. But if we pick the guiding light of our belief in ourselves – our self-love – we will get to our desired destination.

Rick Morrison

Rick Morrison's approach to life can be summed up in one word: Service!

Rick brings an air of integrity, authentic commitment, loving intention and mindful attention to all he does. Along with being an author, Rick oversees a thriving real estate business, wine consulting company and is the guitar player in the band Funkschway. He is also a certified sommelier (and a pretty good cook, too!). Rick has enjoyed prior executive level careers in both the music industry and wine industry. However, none of the above matches the bliss he feels when parenting his six-year-old daughter Shana.

As author of his first children's book entitled, *The Hug Store*, Rick widened his sphere of service to include families, children and fathers everywhere. *The Hug Store* was inspired by a true event that happened to his daughter Shana. It's a beautiful story of self-discovery that illustrates how life's greatest gifts can never be bought, and are instead, always found deep within us.

In addition to blogging, public speaking and facilitating a hugging curriculum in and around the Los Angeles area, Rick has appeared on a variety of talk, radio and TV shows to promote his vision of conscious parenting and ultimately promoting world peace…one hug at a time!

Besides food, wine, hugs and music, Rick's other passions include fitness and overall wellbeing. Rick enjoys charity work and giving back to community. Some other charities that are particularly important to him are Cystic Fibrosis, Muscular Dystrophy, Cancer, Meals on Wheels and Macular Degeneration.

Chapter Two

IT TAKES A CHILD TO RAISE A VILLAGE

By Rick Morrison

OPENING ACT: THE 'STORY'

"The only true reason that you are not happy is the fact that you are in resistance to where you are."
–Kyle Cease

When I began to ponder the question, what if there were some other way to live my life in 2010, the 'knowns' in my world at that time were significantly more frightening than any of the 'unknowns' I might have fathomed. Within a six-month period following the awe-inspiring birth of my daughter Shana, I was diagnosed with an aggressive form of prostate cancer, was laid-off from my well-paying job due to industry consolidation and lost an enormous amount of money selling our house for our cross-country move back to California. In addition, this move, from Michigan to Mill Valley, California, was the seventh time we moved in a two-year period and concluded with our family renting a house, that unbeknownst to us, was a former crystal meth-production facility and brothel!

How might it get any worse than this you might ask? Alas, the beginning of an unsettling divorce, with soon to be co-parents living 350 miles apart, and… a beautiful, wise six-month-old baby girl who was here to illumine the path and change my life forever.

The universe sometimes has an interesting way of waking us up! While at the time you'd think those disturbing experiences would be my 'alarm clock' to wake-up, it was apparently not loud enough. Unexpectedly, it would be my daughter, Shana, who would finally personify that alarm clock, complete with seemingly infinite snooze-alarms that I had no ability to control or turn-off. It was through raising her that my need for control began to dissipate. I learned about a deeper, more meaningful place from which to live my life. By her very existence, she was able to raise my awareness of everything to a new, more vivid level. The mindful awareness that she engendered in me is also a necessary component in raising the consciousness of our planet…and it can be accomplished one village at a time. I realized through the joy and privilege of parenting Shana that it actually begins with me! This was a complete juxtaposition for a forty-five-year old alpha-male, who was now a single father, unsure of his career and clearly in uncharted waters.

With the growing self-awareness that I began to glean from parenting, and Shana along as my co-pilot, I began to realize I could actually accomplish anything without needing the panache and flair which were signature elements that brought me so much success in the wine and music industries. My past 'Story' was just that – a story! It was a learning experience and it no longer defined who I was or how I would choose to live my life. By choosing to reconfigure my mind I began to live more in the present moment, with a child-like awareness. Awe. Wonder. Curiosity. That is where the juice is! It's where creation takes place…and when we are creating, new neural pathways start forming in our brain and more desirable opportunities begin emerging. With my Ego now in check, I realized that Shana was actually here to raise me! It was via her insights, and my awareness of her insights, that we were able to co-author and release our first children's book entitled The Hug Store and co-found The Hug Alliance, a non-profit organization of like-minded, co-collaborators serving to unite communities around the world.

THE HEADLINER: RAISING A SINGULARLY UNIQUE DAUGHTER

"You are raising a Spirit throbbing with its own signature."
    –Dr. Shefali Tsabary

When the movie *The Secret* came out in 2008, my then-wife and I were miserable, both individually and collectively. She thought watching the movie might help snap us out of our despair and unhappiness. I fell asleep ten minutes into the movie! When I asked my wife the next morning what the movie was about, she said it was about being "optimistic and attracting happiness". While that was certainly true on the surface, the movie goes to great depths to creatively articulate how powerful we are and how much 'in-control' of our happiness we really are. I truly needed to hear that message but I guess it still wasn't yet time for me to 'wake-up'.

Around 2011, I began exploring meditation. Like many who begin a meditation practice, I always wondered if I was doing it correctly. In hindsight, I guess I was because it was often during meditation that I began to wonder about the unknown. The real unknown. Where did I come from? What is my purpose? What is my destiny? Meditation enabled me to go beyond my surface mind and realize the unknown was not something to fear, but something rather to embrace. As my meditation practice deepened, I was able to more clearly see my 'victim' mentality paradigm beginning to dissolve. I realized I didn't have to struggle to keep my head above the choppy waves anymore. I was the wave.

I also came across the teachings of Michael Beckwith (Author, Speaker and Developer of the Life Visioning Process - and whom I quote in the Chapter Title). Interestingly, Michael's teachings were similar to the thoughts that had been surfacing in my meditations. Michael's magnetic energy steered me to The Agape Spiritual Center in Los Angeles, California, a joy-filled community that celebrates inclusivity and diversity. Michael inspired me to get-out-of-my-own-way and begin letting go of ways of thinking that no longer served me. I became more open, available and willing in all areas of my life, including how our divorce proceedings went, new career possibilities and how I would ultimately choose to raise Shana as a more conscious parent.

Transformation had begun...

Shana, as all children, are truly here to teach us if we can keep our Egos in check and become aware that every child is a singularly unique spirit. I consider Shana a little Avatar. She may be a child, but she, and all children, are wise beyond their years. Shana continues to be my greatest teacher in becoming the man, the father and the global citizen that I want to be. Children are unique spirits; they are not blank-slates here to fulfill our unmet desires or mold into mini-me's. It is in our lack of self-awareness, that we deprive children of their essence, via our projections onto them of situations and experiences that we have not yet healed from our own childhood.

Shana's first year of pre-school didn't come without bumps in the road. Emergency calls from teachers saying "she might have neurological issues" made my former wife and I think that something might actually be wrong with her. She is quite sensitive and her sensory processing abilities, when pushed to overload, quickly trigger what society calls meltdowns, tantrums and out-of-control behaviors. Testing revealed there was nothing wrong with her. Shana is physically, mentally and emotionally whole. The challenge is that sometimes, intensely perceptive children can get overwhelmed easily by crowds, noises, sudden changes and the emotional distress of others. Criticism, shaming and a lack of connection further widen the divide.

Our culture engineers these labels and categories for children because of the personal baggage we hold deep in our sub-conscious and have not yet examined. Just because a child reacts to situations outside of what society deems normal doesn't mean there is anything wrong with that child. What one is looking at, one is looking with. Shana simply has a highly-sensitive, ultra-strong personality. That is who she is and I freely accept that. Her personality mix can sometimes appear volatile to parents, educators and doctors. However, as I mentioned previously all children have their own unique voices. These sacred voices can help 'grown-ups' become more evolved human beings. The secret is we must consciously choose to listen to them, feel their message, and embody their divine teachings.

A conscious parenting resource that I enthusiastically recommend are books by Dr. Shefali Tsabary. She is an acclaimed author, international speaker and a clinical psychologist. Her teachings are a unique blend of eastern philosophy and western psychology. After reading her book, *The Conscious Parent*, which Oprah endorsed as one of the most profound books on parenting ever written, I found liberation in many ways. In her conscious approach to parenting, "children serve as mirrors of

their parents forgotten selves". Those who are willing and brave enough to look into the mirror have an opportunity to establish a relationship with their own inner state of wholeness. Once parents find their way back to their essence, parents enter into communion with their children, shifting away from the traditional parent-to-child know-it-all approach and more towards a mutual parent-with-child approach. This connection, this yoga, is the path I have chosen in parenting Shana, and in the process, it has allowed me to become more me!

Another tremendous resource is InspiredParenting.com. I bought their brilliant magazine sight-unseen because of the name alone. I wanted to know and learn what it meant to become an 'inspired' parent. They publish a print journal, an on-line magazine and produce a radio show by the same name. The founder, Judy Julin, and her dynamic team are truly inspiring and offer a plethora of creative tools and technologies to assist parents and child care professionals.

Once I began discerning that I was becoming a more awake father, I felt proud when I could detect judgment arising within me with respect to Shana. It was during those moments that I could choose which thoughts to hold about her and any given situation, which often impacted how she acted and/or reacted. There isn't any problem that can't be solved when applying some creativity; children are creative masters…it is their essential nature! Just give a child some markers, an empty cardboard box and come back in an hour to see their masterpiece.

As Dr. Shefali eloquently describes, there is a "clash of time-zones" between children and adults. Adults spend most waking hours thinking about the past or future and very little time in present moment. Children, on the other hand, spend nearly all of their time in the present moment. If we adults would consciously choose to live more in the present, we would experience a richer, more connected, more peaceful relationship with our children. This doesn't mean that parents shouldn't reflect on the past and learn from it, nor that we should neglect important future planning. However, if parents are feeling disconnected from their children, the more time spent in the present moment with them, the more bountiful their connection to them will be.

Here is an example. When Shana was four, we were at a book-store and she was picking out a card for her mom. While writing a note inside the card, Shana accidentally misspelled a word and became very frustrated and agitated. We were in the middle of the busy store with shoppers and clerks all around us. Shana insisted that we buy a new card so she could start over with her writing. I responded by saying, "No, we are not going to buy another card." You might have thought she was being physically tortured by how she reacted when I said no.

As she shrieked, yelled, jiggled, stomped and cried, I took a deep breath as two phrases came to mind: be present and be creative. I knew there would be positive outcome if I remained centered and didn't freak-out at her freaking-out! I had done the inner-work; now it was time to engage and bring that work into action.

I went through my mental check-list: Was Shana in any physical danger? No.
Was Shana hurting anybody physically? No.
Was she hungry? No.

With those answers in check, I knelt down to her eye level, which both empowered her and helped maintain our connectivity. I quickly suggested some possible creative solutions that might fix her writing mistake on the card. The important part was that I was fully present and patient with her as I continued to hold the intention for a creative solution to arise quickly! I noticed little pin-pricks of a shift in her as she began wiping her eyes and I could tell she was longing to let out the smile she was suppressing.

Still though, nothing was working and the situation was far from resolved. Then a few moments later, a sales clerk emerged with a sparkle in her eye and a roll of Wite-out tape in her hand! As I comforted Shana, the sales clerk told her she could use as much of the Wite-out as she needed to fix her writing 'boo-boo'. Eureka! Do less and accomplish more! A creative solution arose, effortlessly, because I trusted and held the intention that it would. By weaving my attention and intention together, we discovered a solution which worked for everyone.

What did Shana teach me? Her experience in the bookstore mirrored and revealed how I felt in other areas of my life. For example, I used to feel a similar agitation and frustration when driving in freeway traffic. What was the point in letting myself get all stressed out while driving when there were more creative things to do with my time and energy? Instead of anger, I shifted my focus to listening to audio books, satellite radio, talk shows, music, podcasts, etc. On days when a nice driver would let me merge, I'd smile back and remember the kindness of the clerk with the Wite-out! The miraculous part of allowing children to teach us is that the results are exponential and life flows more easily!

ENCORE: ACCEPTING THE FEMININE SIDE OF MANHOOD

"The masculine DOES, while the feminine IS"
   —Marianne Williamson

I'm convinced that men who embrace their feminine side are actually more masculine, as they are in better balance and can embrace life more fully. All human beings, regardless of their gender, are born with both inherent feminine and masculine qualities. These particular aspects help define who we are. Our masculine side gets articulated when we're working toward an end goal and continually moving forward. Our feminine side gets articulated when we go with the flow of life, nurture children, embrace creativity, listen deeply and attune to our internal processes. The problem is that because of the collective consciousness of society, many women suppress their masculine energy and nearly all men suppress their feminine energy. This is a fact of modern culture and it's a shame, as we truly need both qualities to thrive and be whole.

Looking back in time, the evolution of men into fully developed humans was due in part to the feminine changes in their bodies over thousands of years. During this time, while men continued to hunt for food, make tools and write on cave walls, their bodies were adapting to the world around them. Their prominent brows narrowed (goodbye unibrow) and became more like the way women's brows were shaped. Their bodies became less muscular. Researchers have attributed this to a decrease in testosterone and other hormonal changes. Homo sapiens became more convivial, compassionate and helpful. We evolved.

It's satisfying to have outlets for both our masculine and feminine predispositions. In our culture, though, masculine qualities – since they're often about progress and moving forward – tend to be valued more than feminine qualities. For men, this can create a feeling of being off-center, both individually and collectively. We are often taught to hold back our tears and emotions even though science dictates that crying is a natural way of cleansing and healing. Many parents, both fathers and mothers, raise their sons to not cry, or if they do cry, to do so in private. Many women wish more men would shed tears and verbally express their emotions. Such women often are drawn to men who can communicate their inner-most feelings.

When we prize too highly our maleness, we spend most of our time striving and very little time resting, taking time off and really connecting with people. When we overestimate masculinity, we become dependent on things, such as technology, cars and gadgets, and we spend less time in nature or expressing our inner thoughts or creative selves. Being overly masculine and under-feminine leaves many men longing for something else. We feel something is missing in us and that we need something outside of ourselves to 'fix' us. But that is an illusion, as reflected by the man who is as discontent and incomplete after getting his dreamed-about shiny new car as he was before he held those keys in his hands. That something else is rarely found and it's a never-ending cycle that we can't quite put our finger on.

For men to break out of this cycle, this means accepting and embracing their feminine energy. There are no short-cuts. Once I began to go-with-the-flow more, connect with my daughter and my inner-self, it made it easier for me to lean-in to life and cease resisting the present moment. Without even knowing it, I needed to experience the feminine side of my manhood to achieve this. I believe all men are seeking to revive their feminine energy; some just aren't aware of it yet. My embrace of the feminine energy has continued to further prosper while parenting Shana.

Shana and all children are here to teach us. They bring the curriculum of living in the present moment and challenge us to awaken so we can become our best selves! With a child as our guide we can truly see life as it is unfolding, in the only moment we are actually living. It really did take a child to raise this awakened, more in-the-flow, more conscious dad. Children truly have the capacity to raise the entire village too, but we must choose to let them. This happens one person at a time and one village at a time. Transformation is progressive. It takes looking within oneself and doing the necessary inner-work. Life truly is an inside job! Thank you, Shana, for teaching me how to Dance in the Unknown!

Joanna "Shakti" Kennedy

Joanna "Shakti" Kennedy founded Ecstatic Intimacy, where she offers programs, events and mentoring to men and women that empower them to put the hot and happy back into love. Joanna says, "There are too many nice guys who 'finish last', too many successful women who can't seem to find a great man and way too many people who find themselves in the friend-zone!" As The Soul Love Mentor, Joanna inspires anyone who hungers for deeper love and intimate pleasure... to find and create a relationship that is an expression of ecstatic authenticity, intimacy and ecstasy. Joanna combines deep experience in masculine-feminine dynamics with her many certifications including Advanced Certified Tantra Educator, Accredited Journey Practitioner, Certified Partner Yoga Instructor and Visionary Leadership Coach. Formally an Electrical Engineer with an MBA, Joanna now lives life to remind men and women of the power and potential of love – showing them how to reconnect with themselves and each other in profoundly loving, deeply intimate and ultimately freeing relationships. You may have seen her as the Intimacy Expert on *America's Got Talent*, or in her other appearances on Fox, VH1, and Comedy Central.

Chapter Three

CHASING LOVE... FIND SOUL...

By Joanna Shakti

We have no idea of the untold miracles that lie in waiting, if we stop fighting our challenges and simply love them. They will teach us, guide us, and lead us to the truth of who we are, to our highest potential and our divine essence.

I only know this in hindsight, as I reflect back on the years of divine synchronicities that blessed my life, turning misery into majesty and pain into passion.

Over those years of miracles, one year in particular stands out beyond all others. Well, it was almost two years, beginning to end, but who's counting?

Let me set the stage, so you can see how this year was so "not" me. I was the precisely planned girl. I was in control and I wasn't a fan of risks.

I grew up in the heart of the 70s, a product of the women's movement, a child of the divorce movement. My model of the world contained beliefs like: Men leave; Never depend on a man; You've got to be tough; Don't let them see you sweat.

To be sure I would never need anyone but me, I got an electrical engineering degree. Yet even though my ego never wanted to need, I craved love. In January of my senior year at Michigan, I met Prince Charming. He was 6'3", blonde haired, blue-eyed, smart, sexy, valedictorian, concert pianist, par golfer and an electrical engineer, like me.

Sadly, I never felt worthy of his love. Yet, if the prince loved me, I wasn't about to let go, even if there were red flags. He proposed in August and I gave up my dream biomedical engineering job because I loved the dream of him more. I sold myself out for love and moved across the country to Houston, took a job in the oil and gas industry and married the prince.

We shared many moments of happiness, for sure, but I wanted kids while he wanted an MBA. We did it his way, working, studying and playing golf together. It didn't matter that he was sleeping next to me; I was sad and lonely. Our sex life was rare and my orgasms even rarer.

Four years later we divorced and I was off again to find Mr. Right. On the professional side, I got promotion after promotion. The money grew, the responsibility and stress grew and happiness dwindled further.

I went through boyfriend after boyfriend, growing more miserable by the day. Finally, after yet another painful breakup, I enrolled in a relationship workshop. That three-hour event ignited my transformation from unhappy engineer to radiant Soul Love Mentor.

Fast forward several months and as the Twin Towers fell on September 11th, I was in Hawaii at "Life Mastery" with Tony Robbins. It was the day the "always-in-control-good-girl" façade began to crumble.

We were stranded as the country reeled. Tony held us and even though many in the room lost family, fiancés, friends and offices, the highest and best thing each of us could do was continue our journey to freedom, awakening and love. My soul awakening continued.

On Saturday, the last day of the event, as Tony taught "Relationship Mastery", something woke up inside me. I didn't understand it yet, and that one moment of scintillating soulful truth would guide and inspire the rest of my life.

My soul took over, aligning with some unknown, unnamed force, a force I'd vehemently denied for years. My control-freak engineer surrendered and allowed my soul to follow the pull of Grace. That day I discovered my feminine nature.

Remember the young girl who thought she had to do it all herself and couldn't depend on anyone? She had no room for being feminine. Yet she quietly cried out to be touched, soothed, cared for and pleasured.

When Tony's event ended, I knew I had to free my feminine soul. I knew I had a purpose. I would ensure that no other woman went through the pain I'd been through and that no other man would go through the pain I'd put men through.

Over the next year, I courted the feminine essence hiding within and gathered every coaching skill I could. I had no idea when I'd leave the corporate world; I simply knew I would. As they say, the stars aligned and I resigned the six-figure career I'd work so hard to build. My friends and colleagues were baffled. I couldn't have been clearer as I looked forward into the unknown.

I filled the backseat and trunk of my Chrysler convertible and put the rest of my belongings in storage. On a Friday afternoon, I began my adventure into the unknown. I thought it would last three months. Eighteen months later I landed 1500 miles away in a state I had yet to visit.

Completely out of character, I started my journey with a four-day silent retreat at a Benedictine monastery in New Mexico. The silence was maddening, confusing and freeing. Looking back, it was the perfect transition from corporate-girl to soul-girl. Then I spent a couple of weeks with a friend in Utah before jumping on a plane to Australia. I planned to visit friends and attend another Tony Robbins leadership training.

After time with friends north of Sydney, I boarded a quick flight to the Gold Coast for the training. Dashing my hopes for extra space and quiet, a man sat down next to me and started talking. Within minutes we discovered that his wife had been a nun at the monastery where I'd just stayed. We had much in common. Before we landed, he invited to his home to meet his wife. My mind thought, "What?! I'm not so sure about this."

He persisted. I relented finally and agreed to visit after the event. He picked me up from the hotel and as we traveled to his house, he asked if I would wait while he made a quick business stop. I waited in the lobby of an architecture office while he met his colleague.

Although plenty of magazines covered the coffee table in front of me, the receptionist, knowing absolutely nothing about me, got up from her desk and handed me a magazine, saying, "I think you'll enjoy this."

Almost immediately an article on cellular healing captured my

attention, advertising a workshop nearby in just ten days.
I thought, *"I have to attend... and how in the world did this woman know?"* I had no answers. I was in awe.

That evening the former nun and I, of course, hit it off. When I shared the workshop in the magazine, she said, "Let's go!" Attending that workshop, and an advanced one, meant I would stay with this amazing couple for nearly three weeks.

Those two workshops inspired the next phase of my adventure. The facilitator asked me to host an event for him in the United States. Thinking that a Tony Robbins event would be a great place to publicize this amazing, Australian facilitator, I signed up to "crew" a workshop in California.

Still meandering in my convertible, I arrived in California with no place to stay. Within the first hour, I'd met another great man who said, "We have a three-story townhome and the downstairs is yours for as long as you'd like." The universe provides.

In California, I made fast friends with a brilliantly feminine woman from Ireland, Judymay, who, by the way, I'd first met in Australia. In our time together, she had one goal – keep me in my feminine energy! She coached me on my voice, my walk, my clothing. I was no longer "allowed" to be masculine.

Sponsoring the Australian workshop seems to have only been Spirit's way of bringing me to California. I let go of that "plan" and Judymay and I headed towards Aspen, Colorado, for another Tony event, this time as participants.

In Aspen, the unnamed guidance took over again. I saw a man across the room and knew I had to talk to him. I had no idea why and my mind raced, "This is crazy." I ignored my thoughts, took a deep breath and came up with a "reason" to approach him.

Of course, divine intervention worked its magic again. His journey paralleled mine and he had "just the place" to take me. The next day, with him as my guide, I had my first profound and direct experience of "God" sitting on a rock in the Maroon Bells.

This man also illuminated where I would be traveling next. He was headed to Florida for a "laying on of hands" training that would be "perfect for me". I thought the idea a little strange but it resonated. I said, "Yes." My convertible took me from Aspen to Houston to Florida that week. Ten days later, I was an ordained minister and my period returned after it had been missing for months. I was finding the world very intriguing.

Shortly afterward, I got a call from Judymay inviting me to meet her at Omega Institute in New York over Labor Day weekend for a spiritual, cellular healing workshop called The Journey. This time I wasn't totally convinced, so I waited for a sign.

I was planning to "crew" my next Tony Robbins event in Denver in July where I would reconnect with Nicki from the UK, the other feminine "guide" I'd met in Australia. At one point, I said, "Hey Nicki, have you ever heard of this thing called The Journey? She laughed saying, "I'm accredited Journey Practitioner and you'd be great at it!" She continued, "I'll fly over from the UK and staff the event. You have to go!"

That was that. Guidance had spoken again and I was going to New York in September. Funny enough, Judymay, who initially invited me, didn't attend. Yet, again, her invite was essential, as that weekend would radically change my life.

The Journey Intensive blew my mind. I had no idea such things existed. I immediately applied for the Practitioner's Program, which included seven courses over eight weeks starting in October, in the UK of all places! Once again, divine providence led the way.

Occasionally, over the course of those summer months, I would fly back to Houston. That's when another 30,000-foot divine intervention happened, but this time I wasn't listening. A man sat down next to me and started talking. We chatted about my journey and the exploration of my feminine nature. I shared my passion and commitment to help men and women uncover their masculine and feminine energy.

The man shared, "I'm in my mid 40's. I've never been married and I want to be. I need your help. Please call me." He handed me his card. I quickly realized he was a VP of a financial services company and, never having had an official client, I immediately thought, "I can't coach him." I put the card in my purse and ignored it.

A few weeks later I returned to Houston to visit a girlfriend. As she and I walked through Whole Foods, the man from the plane walked up to me and said, "You didn't call." I apologized, making an excuse. He handed me his card and again asked me to call. I took the card thinking, "He's too successful. I can't coach him." I didn't call.

I left Houston, visited a few more places and returned about a month later. I was sitting with the same girlfriend at a restaurant on the complete opposite side of Houston, when I heard the man's voice behind me. I thought, *"That can't be him."*

My heart beat faster while embarrassment, awe and humility washed over me.

This time, I tucked my tail between my legs, turned to him, smiled shyly and said, "I guess we're supposed to talk." I took his card and, this time, promised to call. Not only did I coach him, we later shared a two-bedroom apartment in Houston because we both wanted a part-time place there. Oh, by the way, he married the next woman he dated.

You can't orchestrate this stuff. The universe knew what it wanted from me and it made sure I got the message through my think skull, beyond all my self-doubt.

As usual, magic and grace were at work as I planned my UK trip. Nicki would be traveling while I was in England and I had full use of her flat! Was it luck or something greater?

Once in England, The Journey Practitioner training took my mind, my body and my spirit to levels of transcendence, meditation and healing I hadn't known possible. In those six weeks, I left behind years of hurt, judgment, fear and broken-heartedness. I released barrier after barrier in my determination to set my feminine free.

Curiously, before I left for the UK, I had a single date that would again turn out pivotal. I called him midway through my trip. As we talked, I shared what I was experiencing and learning in my training. He replied, "I didn't know you were into all this enlightenment stuff." I replied, "Am I? Is that what this is about?" I had no idea. I simply went where Spirit led. The engineer in me wasn't a believer in "God". But yet, God, the universe, Grace, whatever you want to call it, was now undeniable. This practical stranger, thousands of miles away, had, with just one question, explained my entire journey. I was on a spiritual path, having a spiritual awakening and I had had no idea.

He continued, "If you like that stuff, then I have the perfect spiritual series for you to attend in Austin in January. Come stay with me and we'll sit with this enlightened master." Of course, I said, "Yes" and my next destination revealed itself.

This enlightened master cracked open and shattered more of my barriers to love, waking me up to "who I truly was". Strangely enough, I was beginning to like me, which was a radical change from the self-hatred I'd harbored over the previous two decades. I had such gratitude and awe for everything.

While I was in Austin, I noticed my bank account beginning to reflect my yearlong travels. Of course, the universe provided again.

I got a call from the couple running the North American Journey office, whom I'd met while training in the UK. They wanted marketing help spreading the word about this powerful cellular healing work. They liked me and though I might be the perfect person for the job. I thought, *"Is this really happening again?"* I asked them if they knew I had an MBA in market-ing and they said, "Nope. It just felt right." Somehow, in my hunger, commitment and surrender, I was being blessed with everything I needed.

I took the job and Skip and Kristine would bless my life over and over again in the coming years. As a matter of fact, thirteen years later, my life still intertwines with Kristine's every day.

In Austin, I'm was living temporarily with the fourth man in a year. You might be thinking I slept with all these men. Yet, it wasn't about that at all. In that first year, I made love just one time – a connection that didn't work out – but of course, it led me to a man I would join in relationship.

While sitting at those evening Satsangs (a Sanskrit word that means, "In the company of Truth") in Austin, I met my new boyfriend. He fascinated me with his spiritual commitment and his ability to use NLP (Neuro-Linguistic Programming) to help people lose weight and stop smoking.

He stopped to see me in Houston and we shared a magical dance and passionate kiss in the kitchen. He asked me to join him in Hawaii for a workshop later that week. Of course, I said "yes" and we were off. For the next six months, we traveled, sharing workshops, talking, loving and getting to know the whole power of this masculine-feminine dance of attraction, connection and chemistry.

One of my most memorable moments with him happened while we were driving down I-25 in Colorado Springs, having a bit of a debate. As I was intensely sharing my opinions, I heard Judymay coaching me on my voice and thought, *"I'll try it next time I speak."*

I have no idea what I said, but my guy quickly turned his head and said, "What did you just do?! You're the most attractive you've been in months." He had no idea that I'd simply shifted the energy of my voice and my attractiveness skyrocketed. *"Hmmm...,"* I thought, *"This masculine-feminine stuff really does work!"* What I'd known intellectually was becoming a reality.

We weren't meant to be. After nearly eighteen months on the road, my soul wanted to settle and nest. He wanted to continue wandering.

Wendy L. Yost

Wendy L. Yost partners with individuals, small businesses, Fortune 500 companies and non-profit and educational organizations to grow through change and generate results. With a Master's Degree in Leadership, several coaching certifications and a comprehensive list of speaking topics, Wendy passionately illuminates spiritual principles in ways that leave people inspired to take action. A recent example includes her 2016 TEDx Talk on The Benefits of Learning to Listen to Your Life. As a published writer, Wendy contributed the chapter, Marketing Your Services to Local Colleges & Universities for *The Coaching Code* by Betsy Chasse (2016); the chapter, The Art of Cultivating Professional References, for *101 Great Ways to Enhance Your Career* by Michelle & David Riklan and serves as a Featured Author for http://simplereminders.com, imparting coaching principles through stories for the community's seven million+ subscribers. Wendy is working on two books: One to help children and their parents trust their intuition and another to help female holistic practitioners grow their businesses while navigating divorce. Wendy leads monthly events in Los Angeles every New and Full Moon, weaving her love of nature and ritual with ancient wisdom.

wendy@moreisavailable.com and via moreisavailable.com

Chapter Four

CREATING SPACE FOR MY HEART'S TRUE DESIRES

By Wendy L. Yost

"I will recover my Executive Manager salary in five years – and if not, I will return to Higher Education or get a job in Non Profit Management". That was the promise I made my former husband, and myself, in 2007, when I realized that I couldn't envision another year at the job that I had held for the past five.

Since 2004, I had been coaching on the side and growing ever more aware that the favorite parts of my job involved coaching employees, volunteers and students, helping them identify and achieve their personal and professional goals. The nature of the position I was in, with staff members who had staff members, budgets that had budgets, and meetings that created new meetings, allowed little time to have the connective conversations that I most deeply desired.

This often led to late nights tending to administrative tasks because I had prioritized investing time during the day in support of my co-workers. In May, I hit a breaking point. Staying past midnight to tend to another report that would end up in another binder, I found myself exclaiming to the plants in my office, "I'm moving more paper than people!"

Thankfully a few months prior, my then-husband had moved from working on political campaigns (a rigorous cycle of will the candidate be elected or re-elected) to a more stable government relations position. That meant I felt like I had an opening and that I needed to take it.

"Let yourself be silently drawn by the stronger pull of what you really love. It will not lead you astray."
    –RUMI

I gave three months' notice (something I don't recommend) and used the summer to get my office and files in order, while also trying to download all I knew and had learned on the job into organizational processes that could outlive my working there. August 2007 arrived and it felt like more of a retirement than a career change. I was, as I often said at the time, choosing to grow my coaching and consulting business with greater intention.

My last day was August 15th. I was assisting the handful of clients I had at the time with job searches that were taking longer than expected and life transitions that were proving more challenging than expected. I also had several Department Directors at the university I was departing who expressed interest in hiring me to provide Professional Development Workshops for their employees. It wasn't much, but it was a start. In the absence of my 40-50+ hour a week job, and related management responsibilities, I knew would have new energy to redirect to growing my business.

Here's where things got interesting. Days after going out on my own, I got a call. It was Tom, my mentor from college, with whom I had stayed in close contact through the years, sharing that he was approached about teaching a Leadership Class on campus, that his plate was already too full and that he thought I should teach it.

"The moment one definitely commits oneself, then Providence moves too. All sorts of things occur to help one that would never otherwise have occurred. A whole stream of events issues from the decision, raising in one's favor all manner of unforeseen incidents and meetings and material assistance, which no man could have dreamt would have come his way."
  –William Hutchison Murray

I remember smiling deeply, aware that he was speaking of a Leadership Class that I had taken as an undergrad roughly fifteen years prior. I got off the phone and headed straight to the college archives I kept in my garage. Sure enough, I had the Syllabus and my completed assignments, including the journal we were required to keep throughout the course.

I had minimal teaching experience, having co-instructed a graduate class twice with my former supervisor. I knew what was involved in creating a Syllabus, developing assignments and classroom management, yet I wasn't sure it was sufficient to get hired. I spent hours revising my resume to highlight every presentation ever given and every training and development experience invested in related to Public Speaking.

My mentor arranged for a meeting with the then Department Chair and I arrived in my most "professorial" business suit, newly revised resume in hand, ready to speak to all the transferable skills I had to offer. The Department Chair greeted me warmly and shared, "Here's the syllabus, here's the textbook, here's your mailbox, here's your Copy Code and here's your key. Classes start in two weeks and you have fifty-seven students enrolled." My eyes must have been as big as saucers. I responded with, "I thought this was an interview." He smiled and said, "If Tom says you're good, you're good. Welcome to the department!"

"Stop trying to control your life, it gets in the way of Divine Intervention."
—CHERYL RICHARDSON

What I thought was an ending, leaving a position that at one point was my dream job – and that I eventually grew beyond – had just led to an entirely new opportunity. This new job would allow me to do more of what I loved with fewer administrative and managerial demands. It would also provide a steady source of income while I grew my business. At the time, I knew this was a good thing, but had no idea how important it would become.

What I didn't know then was that university professors, even part time lecturers, are paid year round and can become eligible for full benefits. That part-time job, teaching a class in the Fall of 2007, has since become a core component of my professional life, now spanning ten years of continuous employment. Further, because of the academic calendar, for roughly thirty weeks a year I am accountable for in-class instruction, yet for the remaining twenty-two weeks, I am on break and can focus greater attention on aspects of my business. That phone call in August 2007 was a life changing exchange for which I will forever be grateful.

During my first few semesters of teaching, I was excited about working with college students in new ways. The variety, as the initial class, led to additional teaching opportunities. I also deeply appreciated the sense of belonging that going to campus and engaging in professional activities provided, something that

I would have missed if I worked entirely from home. In addition, continuing on campus in this new capacity allowed me to maintain connections with colleagues in other departments, often resulting in new contracts, some of which were one-offs, some annually recurring and some spanning multiple years.

It turns out, the place I thought I was leaving became my professional home in entirely new ways. Instead of working for one department, I was working for dozens of different departments – leading workshops, helping departments move through organizational change and coaching employees. At the same time, word was spreading off campus about the services that I was now offering as a coach and consultant. I loved what I was doing and the difference I was making. Things were looking good and I was on track to recover my Executive Management salary within the promised timeframe.

Then something happened. Something that I had not anticipated when I gave up my salaried job with good benefits. I needed to end my marriage.

Having been raised in a family where my grandparents celebrated their 65th wedding anniversary, with my parents nearing their 40th, and having waited until thirty five to get married, I was at a total loss that my life, and what I thought it would be, was unraveling.

Teaching became my lifeline. The structure, routines and predictable income provided needed stability as I found myself untethered in an unexpected way. I thought, for sure, I would lose the townhouse that I had purchased prior to my marriage. I wondered how I would make ends meet as the second income I had banked on as part of my plan to recover my salary in five years was about to disappear, and I was just halfway into the time set aside to build my business.

I thought it was quite possible that I would need to move into my parent's house at thirty eight and go back to the kind of job it took so much courage to leave. I was truly grateful for the safety net, but really hoping I didn't need to use it. It was all kinds of awful, as my imagination, which typically resides in whimsy, wonder and awe, turned on me and was now catastrophizing all the worst of the worst case scenarios imaginable. I was in an emotional, financial and logistical tailspin with things getting progressively worse as I did what was necessary to end my marriage and part ways with my then-husband.

I remember wondering, how could this happen? How could this happen, to me? I beat myself up over having left a job that would have made going through the divorce more manageable, at least financially. I felt distant from my dream of having a thriving business where I could make the difference I knew I was here to make and wondered if I was just kidding myself thinking I could create such a thing. Given I am usually a positive person, all of the above was accompanied with running commentary on the running commentary about how I knew better than to believe any of those things (which some days was helpful and some days was not).

"Our prayers are answered in unfamiliar territory."
–Mark Mezadourian

I knew this was more than I could handle on my own, even with incredibly supportive family members and friends. I needed help. I needed a team. In addition to a host of Holistic Practitioners (a Spiritual Advisor, a Homeopath, and a Numerologist, to name a few) and weekly yoga/meditation classes, I was also, at my parent's prompting and with their support, seeing a traditional Marriage and Family Therapist. It was fascinating to see how all these different practitioners provided recurring themes for me to explore and in which to find new footing.

Through their help and that of my family and friends, I started to be able to see the grace that accompanies awful. I learned to trust that my goals, dreams and aspirations were still available; they just might not look like I thought they would. I was also willing to look at how, perhaps, though hard to admit, my marriage was inadequate for the life that I had set out to create.

In addition to hiring emotional support, I also hired financial support in the form of a bankruptcy attorney. When I met with him, again I thought, *"How did I get here?!"* Again I had moments of questioning the intelligence of having left a steady job. Thankfully he had good news. Given my particular constellation of circumstances, rather than declare bankruptcy, something that would leave a black mark on my credit for seven or more years, I had other options.

"Other options" became my mantra at the time, as I did all I could to think in terms of this, or this, or this, or this... – instead of this or that. He encouraged me to try to modify the mortgage on the townhouse (different from refinancing and typically only possible when facing particular hardships) and to settle my credit card debt (versus consolidate it). Both would negatively impact my credit score, but not as significantly or for as long as a bankruptcy would.

The catch? I had to be willing to stop paying my mortgage and credit cards to trigger the possibility of a loan modification and settlements. Having always worked to pay my bills on time, this felt out of integrity. Yet I knew that if I had to forcibly move, on top of all the other changes taking place, it would take me even longer to recover and even longer for me to be of service in all the ways I wanted to be. Countless calls to my mortgage company trying to calmly explain the situation later, I was told about a program that I might qualify for. But that it would involve my needing to submit tax returns, bank statements, anticipated income projections and a detailed letter of hardship.

I had to be willing to ask for help in a new way. I poured my heart into the hardship letter, outright asking for a miracle and disclosing details I'd rather have kept private. I bundled up all the documents requested, over 150 pages worth, and headed to FedEx. On the drive over, slow motion images of having to pack up my townhouse moved through my head interspersed with occasional glimmers of hope that my application would be accepted and that there was a way for this to work.

It took about a year for the mortgage loan to be modified and for the credit card debt to be settled. It was not a fun year. Daily I had debt collectors calling me, trying to intimidate me and repeatedly reminding me of the damage I was doing to my credit and to any future opportunities to work with their lending institutions. What I eventually realized is that when you've temporarily taken up residence in Crappytown, USA, your FICO Score becomes less of a priority. Additionally, once you stop paying your mortgage and that massive hit shows up on your credit score, additional dings aren't nearly as significant as they might be otherwise.

I had to realize that it was not business as usual. Extreme measures were being utilized to move through an exceptionally difficult time. I remember having two post-it notes on my desk: One that read, "Temporary & Manageable" and another that had my name in all caps written largely and under it the word "problem" written in tiny print, to remind me I was bigger than anything I was currently contending with.

Concurrent to all of the logistics I was managing related to the financial fall out of the divorce, which at times felt like a full time job, I was offered additional classes to teach and new coaching and consulting opportunities continued to find me. I knew I was doing good work, making a difference with my clients and students, feeling very well used by Spirit. Yet, despite all that being the case, it felt like my company was being held together by bubblegum and shoestrings.

It was during this time that I started heavily investing in my Spiritual Life, taking classes on metaphysics, intuition and other esoteric topics. As I immersed myself in various teachings, I learned to see my life and my circumstances in more empower-ing ways, more of the time.

My life wasn't perfect, not by a long shot, but I was starting to see the perfection of it. It felt like my Happily Ever After remained available. Perhaps it was actually more available than ever, with my having released aspects of my life and myself that I had outgrown. I have since come to learn that there is an emerging body of research on Post Traumatic Growth (as opposed to Post Traumatic Stress). A quick Google search will lead to related articles, several TED and TEDx Talks and even a Post Traumatic Growth Inventory, all worth exploring to see what factors increase the possibility of growth, and reduce the experience of stress, following trauma.

As these new awarenesses started to permeate my days, new opportunities continued to find me. One opportunity in partic-ular, partnering with a dear friend on a global leadership pro-gram for a corporate client, would supply the income necessary to not only achieve my five year goal of recovering my Executive Management salary, but greatly exceed it.

To this day, I remain in awe of how, with a lot of help in a lot of ways, and the willingness to see my circumstances in new ways, I was able to pick up the pieces of my life and use them to create a new reality for myself.

"All your past, except its beauty is gone, and nothing is left but its blessing."
—A COURSE IN MIRACLES

In my case, creating the space for my heart's true desires required a complete overhaul of life as I knew it and expected it to be. This kind of overhaul is not for the faint of heart and it certainly can't be navigated alone. As I shared, I had a team of people who helped me see what I couldn't yet see, so I could do what I wasn't entirely sure I could do.

Now, a decade later, I can wholeheartedly say I love my life. Sure there are projects to tend to and dreams and aspirations I'm still working to fulfill – yet I know that who I've become along the way is well equipped to meet and move through them all. My capacities have grown to meet past challenges and I trust they will continue to do so moving forward. And perhaps with a little less upset and a little more trust in myself.

Wherever you find yourself today, be it contemplating a major change, in the throes of unexpected change or making your way through the aftermath, know this:

- There is a way for this to work.
- There is more help available than you can possibly fathom.
- Something is being made available through your experience

that wouldn't be available if things were any other way.

For a list of the resources that I relied on to help me move through each of the above stages outlined, visit: moreisavailable. com/dancing. On that page you will find links to the books and poems I read, the classes I took and the movies that inspired me to keep going, along with a worksheet to assist you in moving from *how is this happening to me?* to *this is happening for me.*

In closing, I'd like to offer you the affirmation that resided inside my Medicine Cabinet when things were at their most challenging:

"I move into my greater good always."
    –LOUISE HAY

As so may it be for you. The world needs what's yours to give, and part of your gifts to give arise from who you become as you give them.

Debra Stangl

Nineteen years ago, Debra Stangl was a burned out divorce attorney, forty pounds overweight, $50,000 in debt and in an unhappy marriage. She came to Sedona for the first time and everything changed. As she recounts in her new book, *The Journey to Happy – How Embracing The Concept That Nothing Is Wrong Can Transform Your Life*, $50,000 dropped out of the sky, she lost forty pounds in five weeks (without dieting) and now does the work of her dreams with Sedona Soul Adventures, by helping others find happiness. This year, she became engaged to the man of her dreams, her spiritual partner. The book became an Amazon #1 International Best Seller in five categories and four countries.

Debra was a Family Law Attorney in Omaha, Nebraska, for twenty years (1979-1999). During that time, Nebraska Jaycees named her the "Outstanding Young Nebraskan" for writing and lobbying for the passage of the Children's Trust Fund Act, which funds programs for the prevention of child abuse. A spiritual re-awakening in Sedona, Arizona, in 1999 led her to leave her law practice, and in 2002 she founded Sedona Soul Adventures, which provides life-changing, custom designed retreats for individuals and couples. Last year, Guidedoc named Sedona Soul Adventures the #1 Marriage Retreat in the US.

Learn more about Sedona Soul Adventures at sedonasouladventures.com or call 877-204-3664.

Chapter Five

MY SEDONA SOUL ADVENTURE

*How A Burned Out Divorce Lawyer Found Love, Happiness
and Purpose, by Learning How to Surrender*

By Debra Stangl

In January of 1999, every area of my life was a complete mess. I had just started my 20th year as a divorce attorney and I hated it. I was in an unhappy marriage. Even though my law practice had been lucrative, I suddenly found myself $50,000 in debt because of a failed business venture with my then-husband. On top of all that I was forty pounds overweight. Every single area of my life – work, relationship, financial situation, body – nothing was the way I wanted it to be.

Everything changed when I arrived in Sedona, Arizona, for the first time. I had been on my spiritual path since 1978 when my mother died, but I had never before been to this New Age Mecca that is known around the world. I was doing a session with my practitioner in Omaha, Nebraska, and the information that came in was that I was supposed to go on retreat. The minute that information came in, I heard the word "Sedona" in my head. I didn't even know where it was.

I came to Sedona for what I thought would be three days of

being quiet. Instead my life would change, and change dramatically. This was all because I made the decision to change my life, to take a different path and to dance in the unknown.

Through a strange set of circumstances, I found a tiny retreat center that was up above Sedona in Oak Creek Canyon called "Your Hearts Home". I didn't plan to do any sessions with the owner, Ranjita, because I didn't want to spend the money. Remember, I was $50,000 in debt and realistically shouldn't have even been spending money on the retreat in the first place.

But after I got there, I told her about my situation. For the previous five years, I had been trying to figure out ways of transitioning out of my law practice, all to no avail. During that time I would pray and meditate and say to God, "I'm so unhappy, please tell me what to do" and I would hear a voice that would say, "You need to leave your law practice." But of course I wouldn't listen to that voice. My response was always, "How can I possibly leave my law practice when I'm $50,000 in debt, have nothing in savings and am the sole supporter of the family?"

Ranjita told me, "Your law practice is sucking the life force out of you." She urged me to do a three-hour session with her that was very successful in moving out the old energy and bringing in the energy of transformation.

A little while into the session, my overly-analytical lawyer brain started kicking in and I kept having thoughts of "nothing is happening" and "this was a waste of money". I took a deep breath and relaxed. Suddenly what I would identify as my High Self appeared to me in my mind's eye as the Egyptian Goddess Isis (the goddess who has a woman's body and wings). She enfolded me in her wings and told me everything was going to be alright, but that I had to leave my law practice now. If I didn't, she said, "You're going to die like your mother did."

That thought jolted me to my core. My mother had died at the age of fifty-one after a five-year bout with cancer. Other than the joy she had in her six children, my mother was unhappy, frustrated and dissatisfied. Unbeknownst to me, my father had been having an affair with another woman for many years and my father's alcoholism had reached epic proportions and caused near-financial ruin for our family. I was then forty-six, exactly the same age as my mother had been when she had gotten sick.

Although I had been receiving the message to leave my law practice for over five years, this time I finally got it. Isis' words resonated in my soul, making me finally realize that if I didn't change my life, I was going to die like my mother, unhappy and frustrated.

I went home to Omaha and spent the next two weeks trying to figure out with my lawyer brain how I was going to leave my law practice when I had nothing in savings and was deep in debt. My husband had started a new internet marketing business six months prior to that and we were still in the process of putting money into the business to get it to work, but it was still not profitable.

At the end of two weeks, as I began to feel frustration, I started meditating and talking to God. I said, "I got the message. I truly believe this is what I'm supposed to do, I just don't know how to do it. You've got to give me some help." I went into total surrender. I felt this feeling of peace flood through me. I somehow knew that everything was going to be alright. I didn't know how it was going to be alright, I just knew that it was.

Less than six hours later, I got a phone call from one of my previous divorce clients. At the end of the conversation, out of the blue he told me that he had just purchased a new business refinancing mortgages. I asked him if he thought I could refinance my house to lower my monthly mortgage payment.

He called me back in ten minutes and said, "I can cut your mortgage payment in half, and I can get you $50,000 in cash." I had never told him that I was $50,000 in debt.

Suddenly the weight of five years of financial worry and frustration and fear were gone. But more importantly, I felt like God was winking at me. I had gone into surrender, asked for help and She responded.

I spent the next six months closing my law practice. Nothing to show after twenty years of work, but I didn't care because suddenly I felt free.

I planned on leaving my practice for one year, because I didn't see how I was possibly going to be able to not work for any longer than that.

In May of that year, I went back to Sedona with my husband, Tom, to do a couples retreat with Ranjita. I told her that I was leaving my practice at the end of July and she was amazed and happy. She talked to me about the idea of coming to Sedona for a month in August to unwind from the energy of my practice. I told her there was no way that I could afford to stay at her place for an entire month, but then she kept talking and we reached an arrangement. I would do some basic accounting and tax work for her and sleep on the couch when other visitors would come.

That August was one of the most expansive months of my life. It was amazing being in the incredible energy of beautiful Sedona. I did some sessions with some practitioners I had met through Ranjita. I hiked all the seven vortexes. During that month, she and I became true friends.

Two months later she decided she would buy one of my computers and I would go back there for another month to train her and put her bookkeeping records on it. This started a three-year process of my coming to Sedona for a month at time, spending time in the energy and doing sessions with different practitioners.

Sedona's population is around 12,000 and the spiritual community is even smaller. Within a year, I felt I was starting to become part of that community and people would continually ask me when I was going to move there. I would always answer, "I'm never moving to Sedona. I love my friends in Omaha, I love my house, I love leaving for a while and then coming back."

About mid-way through the three years, I did a session with an incredible practitioner, Raell, who said to me, "Your guides are telling me to tell you that what you are doing now is the most important thing you will ever do." I said to her, "How is that possible when I'm just having fun?"

Throughout the three years, I was doing intense healing work with the different practitioners I was finding in Sedona. There was a particular day when I knew that some major healing had happened. Before Sedona, I had often felt that if I died tomorrow, I would be angry because I had never really lived the life I wanted to live. After spending two years in Sedona doing intense healing work with different practitioners, I was starting to feel a happiness and a peace that I had never known.

One day I was sitting in my kitchen in Omaha, looking out the large front window and watching the huge beautiful trees swaying in the wind in front of me. I was feeling such deep gratitude for my life that I suddenly had the thought that if I died tomorrow it would be okay. Nothing on the outside had happened. I was just struck by the incredible feelings I had on the inside – peace, happiness and contentment.

I continued telling people that I was never moving to Sedona. Never say never. Two weeks before 9/11, I was doing another session in Sedona in the same room I had been in almost three years before. My High Self came in again and told me it was time to move to Sedona. I had no idea why. My experience with these things is that we're never shown the whole thing, we're only shown the next step.

It made absolutely no sense to move to Sedona. Tom was doing well with his work. He was supporting me both financially and emotionally (for which I will be eternally grateful). He had stock options and great health insurance. He wouldn't be able to do his work in Sedona.

The next day I was about to leave Sedona to go back to Omaha. One of my new friends called and said, "I hear you're moving to Sedona. I'm going to India for six months to film a documentary, would you like to rent my house?" Immediately I told her yes and flew home to talk to Tom. I knew he had fallen in love with Sedona too on his visits there, but to my surprise he told me that even though it made no sense financially, he wanted to move there.

Our real estate agent said it would take six months to sell our Omaha house, but we sold it in three days for $30,000 more than list price. I took that as a sign. I knew it made no sense to move to Sedona, but I had reached a point in my life where I needed to do what I was told. I knew I had to take the leap of faith.

Six months after the move I was still waiting to discover what I was supposed to be doing. I said to God, "I did what you told me to do. I moved here, now what am I supposed to do?"

Suddenly, I started having dreams about what would become Sedona Soul Adventures. I saw how before coming to Sedona I had done fifteen years of therapy, read a zillion books and gone to hundreds of workshops and seminars. While all that was beneficial, none of those things had healed me in the way that working one-on-one with the incredible practitioners in Sedona had done. It was the private sessions and not group workshops that had made all the difference. I remembered how I had told certain friends who wanted to come to Sedona, "You should do a session with this person and this person and stay at this place and be sure to have dinner at Dahl & DiLuca." On a very small scale, I was already doing what we do now for our clients. I had found my path. I realized then that my entire life had led me to this.

From the very beginning I wanted everyone to experience what I had experienced – a profound life-changing transformation that would result from working privately with practitioners who could take them from where they were to where they wanted to be. I realized everyone's experience would be different and that each retreat needed to be different.

In my own life, what had caused all the trouble was disconnection--whether on the physical, mental, emotional or spiritual level. When I could figure out what was causing the blocks (what I call "gunk") and clear them out, I could be brought

into connection again. I knew that by clearing out other people's gunk and bringing them into a direct experience of the
divine, their lives would be transformed as well.

Thus, Sedona Soul Adventures was born. We started with
thirteen practitioners, all of whom I had worked with over the
previous three years. We custom designed each retreat and
worked only with individuals and couples. All of the sessions
were private, one-on-one or two-on-one for couples.

The Process works like this. We spend a considerable amount of
time talking to each person or couple, really getting to the heart
of what's causing the problem that's holding them back from joy
and bliss. Then we custom design each retreat for exactly what
that person needs. Individuals are with us a minimum of three
days and couples a minimum of four days, but most people are
with us five days. In each retreat, the people are working privately with five to nine different practitioners who take them
from where they are to where they want to be.

We utilize the three factors that I now call The Sedona Effect:
1) the incredible, transformational energy of Sedona; 2) the
amazing master practitioners who have been drawn here from
all over the world and who know how to utilize that energy;
and 3) the strong energy of desire that our clients bring to
change and transform.

The results are astounding. People come to us burned out,
stressed out, unhappy, depressed, in deep emotional pain and
sometimes feeling like they're at the end of their rope. Many
couples come to us on the verge of divorce.

After going through our Sedona Proven Process, individuals
leave happy, content and at peace knowing their life's purpose

and ready to live it. Couples are able to let go of the resentments of the past, rediscover the love that brought them together in the first place and bring the sizzle back into their relationship. Even after fifteen years and helping thousands and thousands of people, I'm still amazed at what happens.

My own healing continued. I had struggled with my weight my entire life, the result of starting dance at age three and the constant scrutiny and body shaming that went with it. I had been on every diet out there and gone vegetarian, vegan and even raw. It was always the same; as long I was starving myself and doing manic exercising, I would lose weight. The minute I would even think about eating "normal" food again, I would gain it all back and more. I hated my body and I always wanted it to be different.

About eight years ago, the most extraordinary thing happened. When Tom and I would fight, the focus was always on what was wrong with me. After one particular fight, I started sobbing. Suddenly my body started vibrating and after a while I couldn't move. Then I heard a voice in my head that repeated, "nothing is wrong with you, nothing is wrong with you, nothing is wrong with you," over and over. I wanted to believe what the voice was saying, but it almost felt like too much of a stretch. I was overweight and having a serious cash flow problem with Sedona Soul Adventures. But the voice wouldn't stop, forcing me to listen. After a while, I felt a deep and profound calm come over me, very similar to the experience when I had completely surrendered and $50,000 had dropped out of the sky. I knew this was another sign that *Nothing Was Wrong*. Then and there I made the decision to stop the strict dieting and the crazy exercising. I would check in with my body and eat what it felt like eating. Sometimes that would be something "healthy" like a green smoothie, other times it would be an

In-N-Out burger with fries and a chocolate shake! Although this was a foreign concept to me and I had some fears of ballooning up to 250 pounds, the decision felt right. It was time to start loving my body and to stop trying to get it to change.

Five weeks later, I went shopping for a pair of blue jeans. To my amazement, I had gone from a size 14 to a size 6. I went home and got on the scale and was forty pounds lighter than the last time I had weighed myself. Today, I've maintained the weight loss and I eat and drink whatever I want, whenever I want.

The two biggest issues that haunted me my entire life were my weight and my work, specifically not living my life purpose. In both of those situations when I was able to completely let go and surrender, to "dance in the unknown", everything turned around for me.

Tom and I finally split up after twenty years of marriage seven years ago and that brought up issues around worthiness and unlovability that I was surprised to discover were still there. What a gift to have my amazing practitioners help me work through that. Two years ago, I decided I wanted to bring in another love relationship. I'm so happy to tell you that this past March, I became engaged to the most amazing man, who is the most perfect combination of spiritual and grounded that I have ever seen. We are committed to living a happy, conscious relationship and I feel doubly blessed to have him in my life.

If anyone had shown me a video of my life today back in January of 1999, I would have told them it wouldn't have been possible. Back then, I was so desperately unhappy. To have every area of my life turn around has been so phenomenal – to be doing the work of my dreams, to have achieved financial abundance, to finally have the body I've always wanted and best of all, to partner with the man of my dreams. It's all come from being willing to do things differently, to trusting that all will be well, to dancing in the unknown. When I've been able to drop resistance and go into surrender, magical things have happened and continue to happen.

Emad Asfoury

Emad Asfoury lives and works in Los Angeles. As a director, cinematographer and photographer, he has developed a unique style that sets him apart as an artist and craftsman. Emad has traveled extensively and has been working on a panoramic photo book of cityscapes, and landscapes that have helped him evolve his eye for composition and details. His latest film projects are *Duality* with Dr. Deepak Chopra and Don Most (*Happy Days*) and the visually stunning *Egypt Revisited* with music composed by the talented Michaela Eremiasova. Recently Emad went through a divorce, a career change, cancer diagnosis and a new personal relationship. Emad is a believer in personal power on every level – spiritually, physically and mentally. Emad also believes in one human consciousness that connects all of mankind. His belief is that we will ultimately achieve peace and complete freedom when all of us act as one race on a finite planet coexisting with all of its inhabitants driven by love and abundance not fear and scarcity.

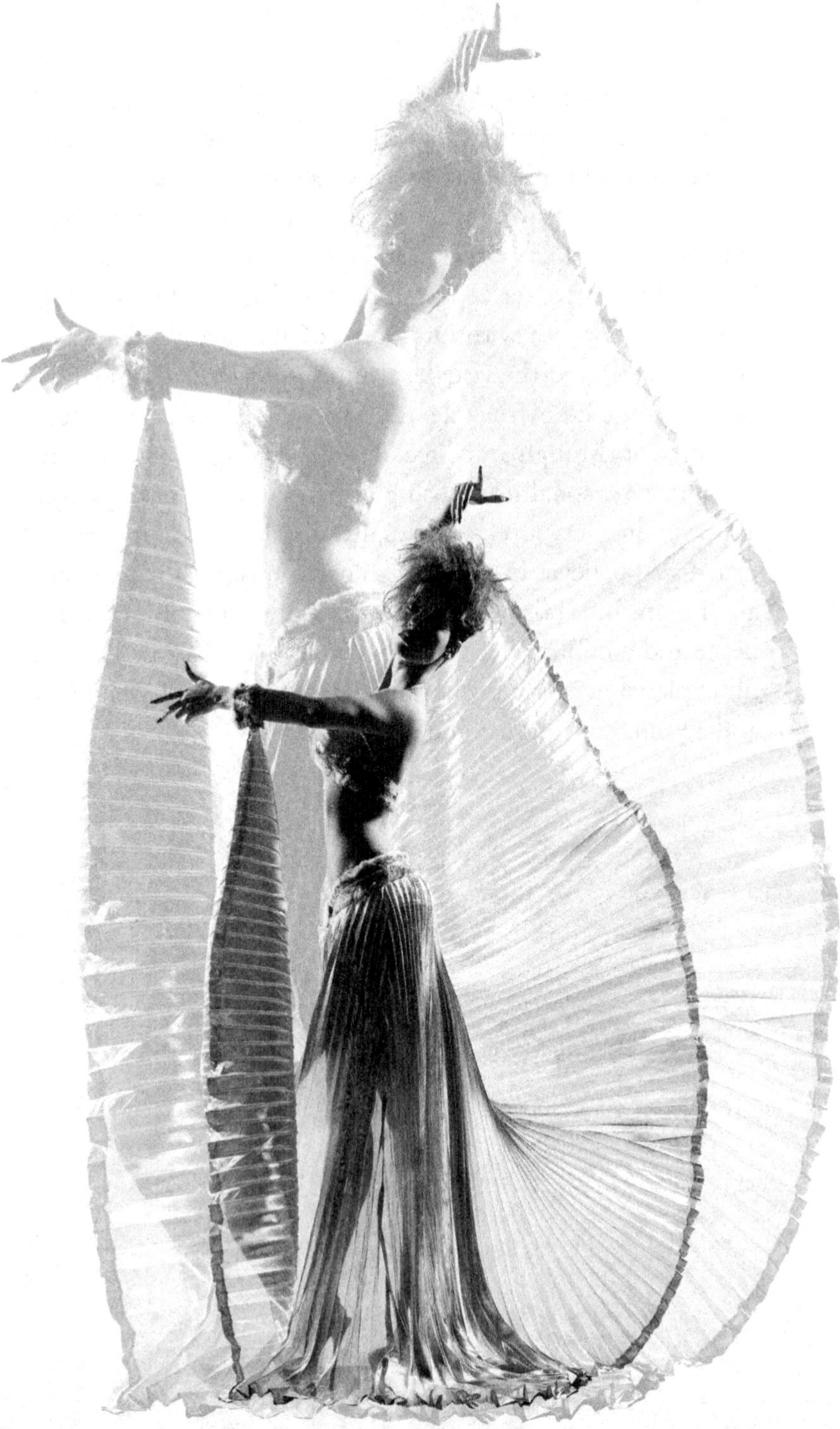

Chapter Six

RIDING THE WINDS OF CHANGE

By Emad Asfoury

This journey spans a few decades. Yet, it feels like a few months. My life has always consisted of a fear element that persistently remained latent or dormant until an event triggers it to the surface.

My family lived an upper Middle-Class life with two kids, a maid, a cook and two nannies. All of that went away on a June afternoon when Israeli Defense Forces preemptively attacked Egypt and Syria on a simultaneous attack that left both militaries in ruins. As a six-year-old, my world was rocked upside down. We began to sleep fully clothed, including shoes, and we spent hours on end in the bomb shelters, after hearing the air-raid sirens that ushered the upheaval to come.

As a grown man, I had forgotten this entire episode. Then the January, 1994, Northridge (California) earthquake brought all my fears of shaking and loud sounds to the surface. That morning I found myself alone in my feelings and had no explanation as of why I had deep fearful feelings from the ground shaking.

I realized that some digging was required and I had to find a link and a cause. You will discover along with me that fear, if left untapped and untouched from childhood, will not go away

and requires a life changing event to compel a person to move passed their breakdown. Join me on a trip faced with failure and demise and see how it all ended up.

THE JOURNEY

It was Memorial Day weekend in 1988. My older brother and I had become proficient sailors, and we had invited three couples and a three-year old to join us on a three-day excursion to Avalon, Catalina, an island off Los Angeles.

We started our sailing trip well prepared with food and drinks. The weather was sunny and the southern California sky could not have looked any bluer. As we anchored off Avalon harbor and settled for dinner and music, we also checked the weather and prevailing winds for the next few days. All seemed to be going well and everyone got along perfectly.

By around 3:00 a.m., I was awoken by wind noise and the rattling of halyards on the aluminum mast. The first thought that came to me was to save our swimwear that was hanging to dry on the lifelines around the deck. I rushed on deck to discover that it was raining and, out of the fog, there was a smaller boat that had lost its mooring and was drifting directly towards our bow.

I sat on the very front of the bow right by the anchor and used my legs to fend off the on-coming boat, but it still managed to hit our bow and chip off a piece of fiberglass. I immediately went down below deck to awaken everybody. The mood had turned sour and grim quite rapidly. My brother and I decided to pull out the anchor and try to "emergency moor" inside the harbor. By the time, we were all up and ready to move. It was right before dawn, and the full scale of the assault was quite evident. This storm had come from nowhere, and surprised everyone, including the Coast Guard that was scrambling to rescue boaters and tug away the drifting boats from the harbor.

We finally made it to the dock at the harbor, and to our dismay, they only gave us five minutes of emergency mooring. Right away, the couple with the three-year-old decided to choose safety and took, as it turned out, the first and only helicopter out of Avalon that day. The rest of us resolved to deal with the worsening conditions and rising swells. The wind intensified and blew at a constant thirty knots (35 mph) and gusted up to sixty knots (69 mph).

As the captain of the boat, all the hard decisions fell squarely on my brother's shoulders. Nevertheless, he opened the discussion to all of us to decide on what to do next. One couple asked to be dropped off at the harbor to spend the night and wait out the storm. The trip back to the harbor was tricky as I had to maneuver through a maze of drifting boats, dinghies and large yachts that formed a barrier to the harbor. As soon as we said good-bye to our second couple and watched them walk further away on the pier, the Harbor Master ordered the remaining four of us to vacate the harbor immediately. I had a dark cloud hover over me despite the clear windy skies. I was so fearful of what was to come I stopped talking, and kept my gaze at the distant horizon.

"Let's hide in the leeward side of the island," my brother shouted. My thoughts were racing, and anything away from the wind was better than nothing. As we approached the southern tip of Catalina, we recognized that we were not the first ones to think of this trick, and that the area was too small and dangerous to sustain a long period of hiding from the wind.

My brother and I looked at each other and said at the same

time, "Let's cross the channel." We had to study the wind direction carefully and see if we could sail northward to our homeport of Marina Del Rey. To find out the direction of the prevailing winds we had to sail away from the island not to have a back draft from the island's mountains and valleys. A mile out to sea gave us a very accurate idea that the wind was coming from the Northwest with some gusts out of the North. This meant that the only direction we could sail safely was Northeast, which led us to Long Beach or San Pedro Harbors.

We started the journey across the channel by going through a safety checklist to make sure we didn't take on water by closing all hatches and tying down any item that could get unhinged in the rough seas. Two miles out, the channel started to feel like a roaring, raging ocean miles away from land. There was no trace of Catalina and certainly none of the mainland. We were feeling the full brunt of the storm. The swells were as high as our mast; this meant that when the boat was in between two peaks we couldn't see past the walls of water that surrounded us. When the boat reached a swell peak, it felt like we were atop a hill in the middle of the ocean. We had limited visibility because of the fast-moving white spray that lifted up from the edge of the swells by the howling relentless winds. We were not prepared for this kind of conditions or the drop in temperature that accompanied the spraying cold ocean water. Soon, my core temperature was dropping, and I feared I would get hypothermic.

Four miles out, the conditions peaked and the water looked black as we started to plow into the troughs of the bottom of the swells. I couldn't get the boat to turn fast enough. I was trying to zigzag my way up the swell closer to the wind. Then right before the boat went off the peak to drop into the next swell, I had to turn quickly on the face of the swell before it could break, to surf down the valley of the swell. Right before

I reached the bottom, I turned yet again to quickly climb up the next swell to avoid any wave from breaking on top of us and capsizing the boat.

It was easy to think of the plan, but despite my best efforts I ran into trouble fast. The rhythm of the waves was changing – getting faster in frequency and higher in amplitude – in such a way that I couldn't stay in synch.

We started taking on water at the peak of every swell as the crest was sheered right off by the wind and scooped right into our boat. At the other end of the valley of the swells, we also took on water when the bow of the boat plowed into the wall of water and spilled dozens of gallons of water below deck. The other couple, who had gone below deck to hide from the elements, found out that the storm followed them and they had no choice but pump water out and use hand held buckets as well.

Twelve miles out, we had settled into a routine of fear and screaming and praying as were faced with wall after wall of water on the way up, and dark, deep waters on the way down. Suddenly, and as I was heading down into a valley of a swell, a peak right behind us crested right on top of us, filling the whole galley and cockpit with cold salty water and sending us facing the wrong way. I thought it was the end. If these conditions persisted, I would not be able to keep up, and it was time to give up on this crossing. I asked my brother to send a May Day out to the Coast Guard to rescue us. Minutes after trying, the Coast Guard responded by asking us to come fourteen more miles to be within a mile from shore to consider towing us to safety. They told us the wind was too strong for a helicopter to fly.

The water inside the cabin was now at least a foot deep. I'd been relying on the engine to help us climb the swells and to navigate the valley turns quickly. As luck would have it, that engine was about to give up on us. A small explosion in the engine room, followed by black smoke, filled the cabin and spilled out into the cockpit. It also sent the overwhelmed couple up on deck and away from the relative safety of the cabin.

Quick and decisive action was required. My brother ordered me to continue steering, while he put out the fire with a fire extinguisher. The cabin looked like a fake movie set with fake white snow covering every surface. I continued to steer the boat up the swells and down the valleys during this mayhem, while thinking that the end is near and death at sea was the only option.

We were halfway into the channel and there was no end in sight. I bundled up in a light sports rain jacket and shorts, which was not enough to protect against the massive blinding sprays and wind.

I felt that there was a hidden hand sabotaging our trip one element at a time. My feelings of invincibility were eroding away with each pile of water that the mighty ocean dumped on us. The boat was lumbering at two or three knots instead of seven to nine knots. It began to feel like the end. We had crossed about twelve miles in about four hours of hard labor. We were exhausted, cold and hungry. None of us had the will to go below deck to fetch food or water for the rest of us; besides most of the food was wet with salt water and fire retardant.

I seriously thought we should abandon the ship, but stopped myself knowing that we would be left for dead with no communications, food or fresh water.

This is as much as I can recollect with vivid details. What transpired next is short of miraculous. The lowest point of the journey is what I always remember and what is vividly projected in front me when I am in tough and dark places.

THE LESSON

Eight months ago, at age fifty-six, I was diagnosed with stage four double mutated gastric Lymphoma. I had sixty days to live if left untreated. I have had a full life, got married, had three kids, started many businesses and stayed in one for twenty-three years, bought and sold many things, including multi-million dollars real estate properties, traveled all over North America, Europe and the Middle East, and yet I wasn't ready to go home. They told me that it was treatable and there was a good chance that I would be cancer free if I completed a rigorous chemo-therapy regiment and Stem Cell Transplant or Bone Marrow Transplant, as it is commonly known.

The first trial was unsuccessful and my oncologist told me that my only choice was to undergo chemotherapy for six consec-utive days at a time, with uninterrupted pumping of the de-bilitating chemicals that destroys the human immune system. Then, the immune system would regain its power on its own for two weeks, only to be destroyed again for six more days. This process had to be repeated until I was cancer free, to allow me to undergo one last step of the Stem Cells Transplant to create a new stronger and cleaner immune system.

Isolated from the process, it sounds easy enough to go through, except it was the most difficult ordeal of my life. I decided to carry on and fight on like I did after the fire on that boat in 1988.

BACK TO SEA

After the fire and the engine stall, we were in dire straits. However, what happened next was no divine miracle or superstitious concoction; we decided to work in unison as a team. My brother worked the main sail to help me steer the boat, while I found new strength in also holding the mainsail line over the winch to tighten it for optimal speed. The poor couple understood that sitting and watching was not a viable option; they continued to pump water and also dried the water off my body and my brother's body to keep us warm. Then they searched for dry uncontaminated food below deck for all of us.

Using only the power of the insane storm wind, we sailed at five knots until we made it to one mile from mainland. The Coast Guard arrived and quickly wrapped us in thermal blankets and gave us hot drinks to warm up our cores. I vowed not to ever sail again, but to my dismay, my brother and I had to move the crippled boat back to its homeport the very next day in very windy, though not nearly as severe, conditions.

The TV news channels broadcast a single shot of our boat from a helicopter hovering above Long Beach, showing how miniscule our boat was compared to the super-size waves. They revealed that our boat was the only sailboat out of six boats that made it back to the mainland. Hundreds lost their boats to the rocky shores of Catalina Island on that day.

CHEMOTHERAPY

As I started my chemotherapy, I lost all fear of death or of cancer, not because I was not afraid, but because I managed what to do and how to fight back. I had decided not to sleep all day in a hospital bed, and forced myself to drag my pump and my weak legs to walk the floor of the hospital eight to ten times every day. I also listed to the news on both TV and radio and talked to my friends on the phone. I sold and bought equipment online to keep me occupied.

My girlfriend also played a significant role in promoting my mental and social agility. We made it a habit to have Shabbat dinners at the hospital room. We ordered cappuccino just to sip the first two sips as I lost my ability to taste or smell and eventually my sense of touch as well. We ordered organic dinners for delivery while we worked on installing and migrating all her files on a new laptop that I ordered online.

I was lucky that I was able to donate my own Stem Cells back to myself and I didn't have to wait for a matching donor. Again, it was digging deeper to find the strength to get out bed after eleven days of very harsh chemotherapy, followed by six days of near death level of fatigue. Eventually I was able to walk a mile a day with hardly any strength in my body.

FREEDOM

Philosophically speaking, fear and anxiety can easily be conquered if you know what's holding you back. However, most people don't see their blind spot or are even aware that they have one. Mankind evolved to have inner fears as an indicator to decide whether to fight or to flee. Even though we don't face these mortal dangers in our daily lives anymore, our reptilian brain has not evolved to jettison these primitive emotions. We have to learn to upgrade our firmware to keep up with the times. It is easy to see an actual situation where fear and anxiety are not abstract but real as in fear of drowning, or fire, or even bullying. When the situation is more symbolic such as fear of change, or fear of technology, or best of all, fear of success, we would discover that if we equate the word that we are afraid of, to one that comes out of our ancestral evolution such being eaten or drowned or even burned, the result is clear.

Most of us through training and science have developed a strategy when faced with, for example, a mugger. We either give him what he wants or run and scream for help. When faced with drowning, hardly anyone will stand still in the water until they're completely out of breath. When faced with fire, most of us will run in the opposite direction and only those who are shocked or caught at the wrong time at the wrong place will perish. My point is, once a danger is identified most people will act and defeat it.

But our modern lives disguise danger and present it as a food, boring work, low wage, a bad relationship or empty bank account, etc. If we have the quick ability to distinguish the danger in these aforementioned dangers, it's possible to do something about it long before it festers. Most humans do not perceive food as dangerous until it is too late, the same with dead-end low paying job or useless unhealthy relationship. As matter of exercise, one should learn to identify one's fear. That's to say, the sooner we recognize a behavior or social element as danger, the easier it is to eradicate the danger. We need to elevate the status of the elements that we are afraid of to mortal danger rather than lower their status to insignificant matters that do not require any action. This way we are compelled to act swiftly and vigorously against everyday events while they are small moguls before they become mountains that can topple us in our tracks.

YOU ARE IT

The single motivator that will change your world is YOU. The difference between you today and you ten years from now is what you do for yourself in between. There are no rescue boats in the middle of the ocean, but there is you and your ability to harness the wind. Recognize that all those external powers that may control your life such as God, Nature and Society are all inside of you as well. You are a microcosm of the universe.

"You are not just a drop in the ocean, you're the mighty ocean in the drop"
  –RUMI

Wendy Keown

Wendy Keown is a wild and devoted student and teacher of life. Since very young, her eagerness to explore any and many traditions has led her to deeper spirituality, personal freedom and her own authenticity. She has learned from and taught alongside many prominent teachers, and has led her own private classes and journeys. She produced the documentary, *The Empty Womb*, with Betsy Chasse. Now, her wanderlust may find her almost anywhere on the planet, immersed with the locals, a shaman or on a pilgrimage. You may catch her scribbling on anything, anywhere. She is currently working on her new book, *Enough, Already – Five Life Vows to Personal Freedom and Living a Wild, Authentic Life*. When her nomad spirit needs renewing she loves, laughs and plays with her husband of thirty years, family, and friends in Lake Tahoe, California. Her life motto: pray, play, and stay, In Love.

Chapter Seven

DANCING WITH ABANDON

By Wendy Keown

How can we know the dancer from the dance?
   –W.B. Yeats

I didn't even see the end coming of this twenty year apprenticeship with my teacher and master. Actually, it was really the
beginning not the ending.

My pink slip read, "I will love you always, the student has become her own master. Have a nice life." With profound compassion I was shown the door out. My apprenticeship wasn't really
over. It had most assuredly just begun. Was I scared? At first,
yes, terrified. Were these experiences all just another mask? The
great pretender had shown me still pretending. The great image
I had spent a lifetime creating, defending, becoming enough, lay
crumbled at my feet. All my training, all the wisdom, seemed to
tumble and whir in my mind. A million pieces like those shattered on the ground. I could never be put back together.

But that was what I had wanted – to see the false masks. Under each mask another false self had fallen away, like pulling a
thread from the back of a tapestry. Slowly, I unraveled, as the
string of faith was pulled from each belief, painfully, one by
one, layer by layer.

The house of me was burned to the ground. I wasn't homeless, but it felt like it. All that was salvaged was my true self and she embraced herself for the first time in her life. Like a phoenix she rose from the ashes. I felt raw, new, exposed and loved. I had freedom to create and live my own life. A new book opened, white and empty, waiting to be filled by my pen, in my hand, and with the story of my choosing.

The Whitney Houston song *I Wanna Dance With Somebody* came into my head. The lyrics and melody drifted through my thoughts, *"When the night falls, the loneliness calls, I wanna dance with somebody, feel the heat with somebody, yeah, with somebody who loves me..."* A tear ran down my cheek because I realized most of my life I had spent looking for that somebody, remembering that on my tenth birthday I wished for a prince to ride in on a horse and save me. I would do anything to please, giving up myself and changing who I was to fit in and receive that love. I wanted to be seen, acknowledged, approved of, and practice to get the steps right to be eligible to enter the contest of life. Then I just wanted to stay in step with my teacher. To be his best student. To have him be proud of my ability to follow his lead.

I was self-conscious because I'd believed all the people who told me I wasn't a great dancer. If I was cajoled into joining a line dance, I soon stepped out, convinced I'd thrown everyone off. "Better to stay seated," I lectured myself. Or practice, practice, practice, until I was good enough.

For a long time I even resented my husband because when we first met he knew I loved dancing and we went dancing all the time. We even took salsa lessons and went to salsa clubs. Then, after we were married, we just stopped going dancing. Every once in a while, my mind would let go and I'd let my body move to its own rhythm. Then I'd remember my failings and stop in mid-step and wait for my husband – a good dancer – to lead.

I loved watching dance scenes in movies. All of the best ones seemed so natural. Spontaneously, they would just break out in a free form, natural dance: *Footloose, Saturday Night Fever, Flashdance, Risky Business, Singin' in the Rain, Love,* When was the last time I had felt like that? Uncaring about others opinions. Just alive, full of joy, loving life! Not often. Not often enough.

I reflected on moments of exquisite dances with my teacher. Now he was the great dancer, leading me effortlessly around the floor and lifting me off my feet in perfect time. Even then, I was, at times thinking of how wonderful it looked to others, how perfectly we flowed, how others might envy us, as we moved and glided in sync to each other's slightest movement of the hand. I'm sure we looked flawless, in perfect time. But, as always, even this was a teaching.

Now, I see how my ego loved being his special student. I had finally been chosen. I had dedicated myself heart and soul, again to another. I stepped out, risking everything dear to me. Willing to give up anything to learn this. He wasn't much different from the men paid to dance with the ladies on a cruise ship. He saw my willingness and desire to learn, to be guided, to give him my trust and authority. He made me look like a great dancer and I believed I could never look that good without him. That was my fear. Would I ever be good enough?

It seems in looking back it was like a death, a literal dying to my old self. I was familiar with the stages of death and its passages in my job as a hospice nurse and giving end-of-life care to my own parents, family and friends. This was different. This wasn't just close to home. This *was* home. I went through all the stages in differing degrees at the beginning. Denial, anger, bargaining, all mixed in with my wounds. Everything surfaced. Along with it the grief of losing this identity I had so carefully built over a lifetime to protect me and help me survive.

I had always built myself up as the good girl. I could read fluently before I went to kindergarten. I was the first in my family to get a college degree (actually, three degrees). The good student, mother, friend, daughter, boss, wife and on and on. It was never ending and exhausting. I was the adult child of a whole family of alcoholics: A borderline personality disorder mother and four fathers I never knew. I could never get it quite right or the expectations would change or I would judge it as not enough. There was always someone or something to blame. If only they would change. Why couldn't they hear my silent scream of "enough"?

All I could say was, it was a "good effort". Stopping in the middle of the floor, still spinning in a dizzying swoon from the tug of war and two step of my mind and heart, I firmly and lovingly said, "Stop it!" The ranting slowed and quieted as I recognized the steps I'd been practicing forever. I yearned to conform and followed all those rules: Stay in step with others; it's not polite to step on others toes; apologize; get along; don't make waves; fit in; when everyone moves right, move right. All the familiar patterns. My feet moving effortlessly, to uncertainty, doubt, guilt, more, more, more. Higher, better, longer, faster. "Stop, slow down, you don't need to know. You don't have to get it perfect." I whispered.

After years of working on myself, thinking I had finally been given the equivalent of a diploma by this master, I had graduated to a new level of happiness and transformation. Oh yes,

I was more aware. Now I was acutely aware of the waltzing around *enough*. It seems I hadn't quite made the ascended honor society I had aimed for. I flailed about, a fish out of water gasping for air.

As he closed one door, the door of uncertainty and fear opened. Once again. I could hear his gentle voice saying, "You don't have to be good." Still the questions, depression and loneliness came rushing in to fill the void. This was the dance contest I had been practicing for and I was still in rehearsals, forever the understudy. As I worked through the resistance and grief, slowly, small bubbles of freedom, acceptance, and happiness resurfaced with me. They had always been there, tied by the anchor of my doubt, guilt, shame and insecurity. He showed me the chain of false beliefs I followed to the very depths. There at the bottom of my heart lay all the illusions and lies that held me fast. They were strong because I had given them all my power. All my faith.

My mind went into reaction and fed on my fear. I had been immersed in love, peace, play; the racing thoughts felt not only foreign but like the web he had helped me see and destroy was being just as rapidly rewoven by my cunning spider mind. What I had only named my thoughts of fear and doubt, my "Spideysense" was now not humorous. I did my best to quiet my mind and remember his words. I wanted desperately to run back. I wasn't ready. I needed his wisdom. Or so I told myself.

I needed to calm the panic and to find the connection that felt the all-encompassing love again – the deep love that, like an unpierceable veil, had cloaked me and warded off all doubt. I felt only abandonment. Again. Or so I lied to myself. Caught in my own sticky web of lies. Gently, like talking a jumper off a ledge, I began to feel my own self love and acceptance, calming the cacophony. My mind quieted as I came back to present awareness. Slowly I was starting to remembering the sound of *my* true voice.

Now I was on the dance floor alone. I was swirling about in a dizzying two step while my heart was taking two steps forward and my mind one step back. "Well," I heard his voice echo, "what makes you happy, honeydew?" It had been so long since I had asked myself that question. With him I just flowed in the moment. Not questioning, following, trusting, loving, learning, listening. Hanging on every word and action.

"You know what to do. Listen to your truth," I urged myself. "Listen to your heart, only your own heart has the answer." My mind shouted to pick up the pieces and try to glue myself back together. The broken structure and masks at my feet were just that. They didn't need repair. I had pieced myself, heart and soul, back together and soldiered on throughout my life, through hurt, anger, resentment, betrayal and abandonment. He hadn't abandoned me. He had set me free. I *was* free – free of all the opinions, the judgments, good and bad, right and wrong, guilt and shame. I was free to remember I was enough. This was the part of me that was true and I held it tightly, like a touchstone. I had always been good enough. I vowed to myself, "I may forget. I may lose my footing. I may stumble, but somewhere inside me knows I'm enough."

I had no idea what or who I was. There was just "I am". I remembered the feeling of dancing, floating, across the dance floor of life. I could never be a wallflower again. He wasn't the prince who had woken up sleeping beauty. That was part of the final lesson. Like all fairy tales we would not dance and dine till the end of our days together in the castle of happiness. No one can wake another up. There are those masters, shamans, gurus, like him, who could give me an experience and reflect love and pure joy. But that was all it was, a reflection I could not see of what was always in me. He had held up the mirror of my own Truth for me to see clearly. A mirror of *My Truth*, not his. It ached for the return to my own love, my own kiss to wake me, my own arms to hold me. This was the Great Love I had been searching and searching for. I had to unchain my heart. This was a returning not a beginning. The Great Love waiting to hold its beloved, long lost child.

I had never been abandoned as heartlessly and carelessly, as I had abandoned myself. This life was my dance to be danced in my own way. No one else could dance it for me or hear the music my heart sang. My story was like all heroine's journeys. I had refused the call many times. In all the tall tales you had to leave your ordinary home to a new and unknown world. I heard the small quiet voice calling me to the great adventure. The call answered, the door opened, as it always does if you dare to ask. But I had to ask. A sure and wise hand welcomed me across that threshold. Yes, the door closed behind me. Fearing what would surely be a deadly path. The One Light lite the way and the path appeared. As I journeyed, all along the way allies, partners, teachers, friends, tricksters, and wise men pointed the way. All paths led home, no matter the teacher. Only I could save my own world. Bring home the elixir, pull the sword from the stone, wear the ring of power. The seizing of my own power and strength was mine to give away or take back. Waiting for my vow of allegiance to honor and cherish myself forever.

I took a sacred vow never to forsake myself again and to honor my own happiness. I pledged to be the one I could trust to love myself unconditionally and to accept without judgment and with forgiveness all of my past, present and future. I could depend on me to step out on the great dance floor of life and to swoon with her own divine, ecstatic, amazing self. I had to be shown the gift of my own true self and power. In the myths and fables the characters are one and the same. All parts of the One Self. Feminine and masculine strengths to be merged, blended. I was the rescuer and the rescued. I was Beauty and the Beast, Harry and Dumbledore, Luke and Yoda, the master and the teacher. I was the master I was looking for. Everyone and event in my life was my teacher. Each one a reflection of my thoughts, actions and beliefs. I *was* cause. All stories were *my* story. What I knew I wanted was to continue that beautiful dance of life. Content and confident, without care of what anyone thought, how I looked, including myself. I could continue to have that feeling but how would I sustain it out in the world. My ordinary world I had chosen to return to and those I loved in it. Now I would return with new eyes open and with the perception of love.

It was up to me to find a way, my way, to ignore the judges, the jeers, the critics of my style. But, I vowed to listen to my heart and let it dance. This was *my* dance, to *my* tune. To worthy to dance with a master was no longer important as I realized I was already enough. I had always, innately, known how to dance. I could always, anytime, dance with somebody who loved me when I loved myself. I would always keep my dance card open.

It was then I remembered that I knew this truth once. At the end of a spiritual journey years ago, a band was playing in the small lounge and I was just simply in love with the world, with me and "in the zone of love". I'd danced for hours by myself, with other women, men, just flowing, my heart open, skirt twirling. I'm sure I glowed. Smiling, laughing, spinning. I was *In Love*.

Another time, I was on the small island of Santorini in Greece sitting at a quaint little outdoor restaurant overlooking the sea. The small band started playing and without thinking about it, I just got up and started dancing. Singing Opa! and holding my hands high clapping and snapping. I was in heaven. I was authentic. That was what the word *felt* like. It was a way of being that came from a way of feeling. I felt *free*, in joy, in the moment, my mind was not judging or criticizing, it was quiet, absent.

I had allowed myself to forget those incidents, but I would not make that mistake again. Ever.

It could no longer be hidden. It was my Truth. I knew when true awareness came to me crystal clear and without reservation. I had no doubt, no uncertainty, and most importantly, pure love and acceptance. But it required removing my faith from false beliefs and being responsible for my perception. It was up to me to choose the feelings I wanted to experience. I could choose how I would feel, react, respond, interpret and perceive all events, and mine and other people's actions and words. Even if I wanted a dance partner. I no longer needed one. That was the difference. I was enough. From this moment forward I was at choice. I had an awareness I could never lose, that was there whenever I chose to remember it. Like musical chairs, I could forget for years but as soon I chose to remember, it would all come back. The music playing was irrelevant. There was no winning or losing. A grand game of my choosing, where, what and with who. My playing piece free will. It was my dream. I could always choose to merrily, merrily, row my boat down the stream. What I wanted now was just to dance. That epiphany brought a huge smile to my face.

I want to dance with wild, fierce abandon and be fearless, spon-taneous and fully alive. What I know now is the more I do this the more it just comes naturally. The sweet innocence returns and I can flow with life with whatever rhythm plays.

The love, acceptance and approval I desperately wanted was my own. I was the dance partner I had always been looking for. I bowed to myself and I began to dance with abandon.

Peymaneh Mokhtar Rothstein

Peymaneh Mokhtar Rothstein is a film producer with a vision of creating extraordinary, social-conscious films with a message. Through her production company, Leap4wrd LLC, of which she is the CEO, she does exactly that.

Ms. Rothstein grew up in Iran during the Iran-Iraq War. There she witnessed immeasurable destruction caused by bombings in her hometown and as close as her own street. It was through her survival in these dangerous times that Ms. Rothstein developed her steadfast belief that "life is a precious gift". This belief continues to touch everything in which Ms. Rothstein is involved. Aside from her filmmaking ventures, Ms. Rothstein founded Precious Time Centers in July of 2001, which provides on-site childcare facilities at corporations across the country.

As a professional woman and mother of two young daughters, she understands firsthand the challenges of finding the balance between work and family. Ms. Rothstein strives daily to serve humanity through fostering strong family bonds and enriching the lives of her own children, and children everywhere. A results-oriented person with great determination, Ms. Rothstein sets ambitious goals and achieves remarkable results, not just for herself but for the benefit of all those whose life she touches.

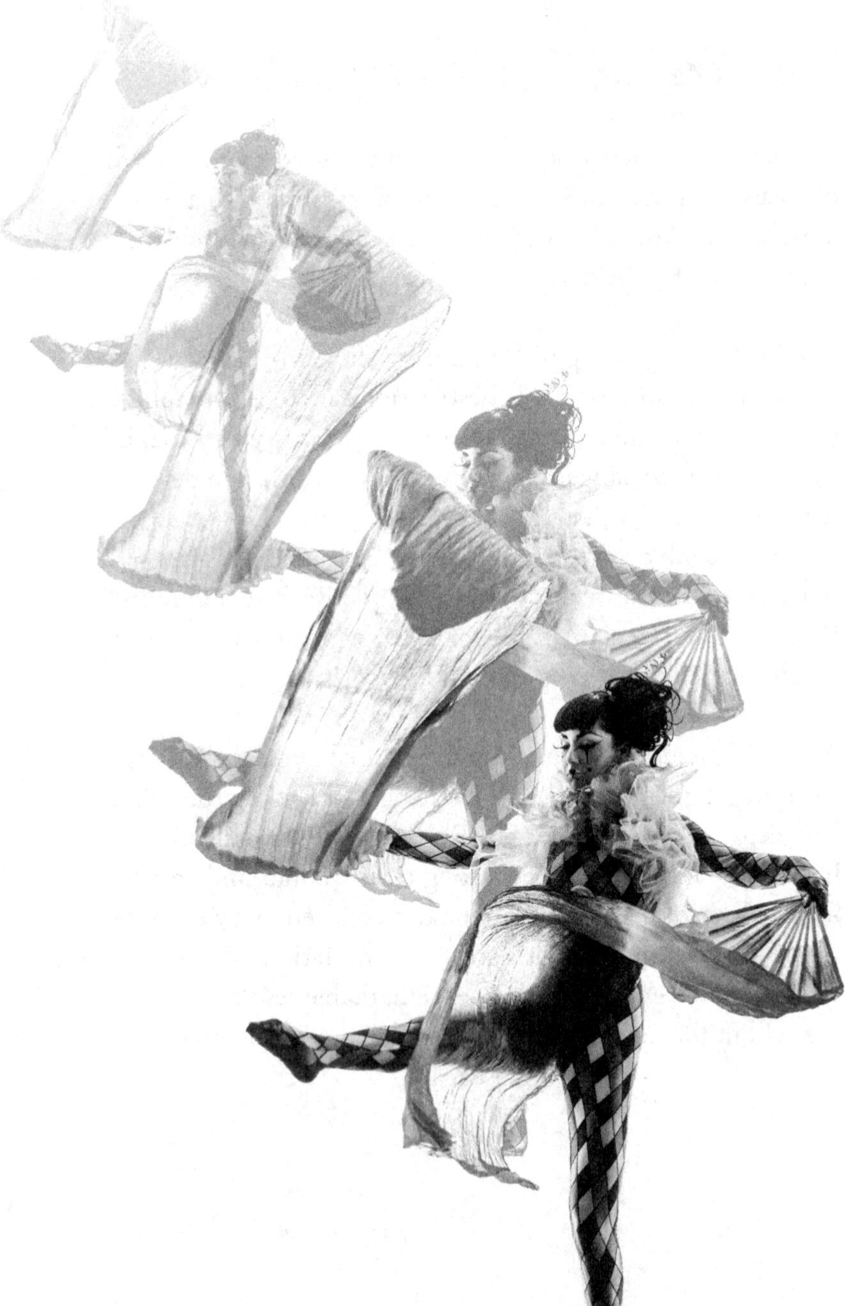

Chapter Eight

TRIUMPH IN SPITE OF DOUBT

By Peymaneh Mokhtar Rothstein

It's the summer of 1985 and I am nine years old and living in Tehran, Iran. It's a night like all the other nights I've known living in my country, which is in the middle of a war and where our "enemy," Iraq, drops bombs on civilians. I'm staying with my grandparents while my mom drives to another city to pick up my brothers. There is nothing out of the ordinary about this; ever since my mother and father divorced there are a lot of these back and forth trips – picking or dropping off – my brothers and me. Like I said, it's a night like all the other nights of my life. Until…

The sirens blare. The lights shut off. We head downstairs, seeking safety underneath the staircase. We're not alone; all of our neighbors in the apartment building are heading downstairs too. Twenty kids are rushing down while twenty adults are trying their hardest to keep things light by making jokes. I hear laughter – nervous laughter – as loud as I hear the sirens and the sound of all our feet hurrying.

For some reason instead of going downstairs, my grandfather goes outside and into the yard. In an instant, I make the decision to go with him. While standing there with him, I look up to see airplanes flying over us. All of the sudden the sky turns red, and I know this is not normal. But my brain can't process this because immediately after I look up there's a thunderous explosion. Then there's another thing that doesn't make sense and isn't normal: it's a feeling of being thrown, and then of flying across the street, while below me there's a scream that seems to go on forever.

I awake to more screaming, to fires and to a panicky feeling because I don't see my grandfather. I think, "Everyone is dead and I'm alone." All these years later, writing that sentence still makes me gasp, and I have to catch my breath. I feel like I'm back in 1985, back on my street and feeling that terrifying feeling that life, as I knew it, was over.

It was a stroke of luck that we didn't lose a single person in my family, despite the destruction and death all around us. I realized the very next day that many children were killed at a birthday party and many families were divided and broken forever. Seeing their body parts and our devastated neighborhood remains a constant visual in my mind's eye and a constant wound in my psyche that has never left my soul.

The young nine-year-old was now faced with the heavy knowledge and guilt that the bomb that hit our building didn't explode yet others right next to us exploded and killed our neighbors. This defining moment was when I first asked those questions, "Why me?" and "What's the purpose of my spared life?" I felt responsible for protecting the young innocent children's lives and this went on to define my adult life.

Since that day, I realized how fragile my life is and how thin the thread is that it's hanging on. My life's been one unknown after another. Yet it's always been driven by one huge known: that my soul and spirit are here to live a life with purpose... passionately. I survived a war. My life was a gift and I knew it. Now all I had to do was find that purpose – my purpose – for being alive.

Flash forward to the winter of 1989. My brothers, my grandmother and I have escaped out of Iran, and are headed to magnificent America. Or so we think. First there's a stop in Vienna, Austria, to get our final paperwork in order. Then, following a conflict with my grandmother, I moved out and stayed in a place with teenagers who were brutally unkind. Every day, I babysat, doing it as much to make a living as to keep myself busy while the time dragged by. Seasons moved from winter to summer, and finally we got permission to enter America. A new chapter began.

I moved to Los Angeles and earned a university degree while supporting myself financially, as I had done since I turned seventeen. I moved along and upwards in jobs: bank teller to bank supervisor, to producer on a radio talk show where I had access to interview amazing people. Each person I met impacted my life. Each position I took opened a world not just of knowledge, but also of understanding.

Although I was living life, and I was also still living under the darkness of my childhood trauma: war, abuse, and being uprooted from a world that was all I'd ever known. Yet what was also becoming more and more clear was that while I was not in any way in control of my past, I was absolutely in control of today, and of my future. What I chose to do with my life, what actions I committed to... all of it was totally and completely in my hands.

I took advantage of an opportunity to register for a business seminar promising to help discover and develop my gifts and business ideas. Halfway through the first day of this wild dance into the unknown, my turn came to present my passion to the group. I'd known since I was nine that my passion was to protect children, but I'd had no real idea where to take it. I was thinking: *Isn't this was why I'm here? Because I'm twenty-four and I'm tired of not knowing what shape my passion would take?*

Then something happened. Out of nowhere, I flashed on a TV piece I'd seen years earlier of nannies caught on hidden cameras, abusing the children they were in charge of keeping safe. In that instant, a full vision of what my work would be presented itself. I would establish on-site daycare centers at the corporations where parents work. At any time during their day, they could stop in, see their kids, see that they're under good care, see that they're happy and, of course, see that they are safe. In that moment, I felt molecules in my body shift and align such that I was clear this was why my life was spared. This was the inception of *Precious Time Child Development Centers* as I believe every second with children is precious.

However, the idea was just that and I had no idea how to turn it into reality, no idea how to start a business. But driven by my love for children and my clear vision of what my passion and purpose for being alive looked, I started creating a plan.

First, I asked a friend to be my coach, to help me create a game plan and take concrete action. I also started sharing my vision with anyone and everyone I met. I became a human sponge, soaking up every little bit of useful knowledge I could uncover. Finally, since I didn't want to just dance in the unknown but to dive into it, I took the radical step of quitting my job in order to devote my entire focus to building my vision.

Fantastic times. Exciting days. I was focused and moving. But the bills kept coming in, and my mortgage was due and I was plagued by how I'll pay for everything. Yet I also felt uplifted and recommitted to my purpose every day.

One afternoon I opened a letter from my condominium home-owners' association asking me, *"How would I like to receive my $10,000 settlement from the Northridge Earthquake?"* For one moment my problems were solved! That was followed by the next moment, when I knew they were not. Because as much the money matters, I know I have to tell them I wasn't the owner when that earthquake hit.

I called and then got the most pleasant surprise. They told me the money belonged to my unit, and since I was the owner now, the money was my money. At that instant, I understood that integrity and honesty matter more than money, possibly more than anything – other than love.

This was a sign that I was on the right track. Free of money issues I moved into a new phase of my business. My creativity was sparked daily by the awareness that I was moving closer and closer to fulfilling my original vision. I was thinking big and dreaming bigger. I realized that my first corporate client had to be a big one, big enough to establish my credibility. Driving in Los Angeles I passed by a Kinkos, and I saw it: They would be my first client.

I still didn't know how this was going to happen. First step was research. I focused on the founder and incredible entrepreneur, Paul Orfaleo, and I knew I wanted to meet him. I also reached out to many different organizations to seek partnerships. The results were discouraging: *"You should start with something smaller,"* *"You don't have any experience,"* *"Your business plan is too much for a young woman."* Even my own family told me to get a job and stop wasting my time. Each negative comment felt like a huge slap in the face. Like that night long ago when the bomb struck, I felt completely alone, except for my coach. He seemed to be the only one who still believed in me.

My coach also reminded me that I was the one with the power to make things happen. I realized that had to make it happen soon because once again my money was about to run out. My fears rose to the surface: *"How will I pay my mortgage? What will I do for food, and my basic needs?"* Then I noticed something else: Not all the fear was mine. Some was coming from my family. Some came from potential investors who looked at me with amusement and then suggested that I get a sales job since I was "so good at it".

I couldn't do anything about the fear of others. But in order to move forward, I had to get a clear understanding of my own fears. I had to understand what belonged to me. I started to see that I had very basic survival/safety fears and very clear money fears. To make the money fear dissipate, I took a job to restore my financial integrity. Yet all the while I never stopped searching for a connection to Kinkos, and I never stopped talking to potential investors. I was constantly trying to create new partnerships.

On week two of my new job, I woke up with an urge to search the internet to find someone connected to Kinkos. Within five minutes I came across the name Cynthia Kersey, who is the author of the very inspiring book, *Unstoppable*. Not only was her book being sold at Kinkos, but Paul Orfaleo wrote the endorsement for it! I sent her an email via her website, with a quick introduction of myself and my vision for Precious Time, then without hesitating, I asked for her support. Less than twenty-four hours later she wrote back, suggesting we meet that week. My amazement turned into awe of this remarkable woman. She wholeheartedly offered her support, and set up a meeting for us with Paul Orfaleo. Divine certainly knows exactly how and when to orchestrate the right time for us to meet because Paul was going through a buyout with Fed-Ex, and was looking to outsource their childcare center. With a solid chance to have the contract, my coach and I set out to create a new business plan, which included the addition of childcare experts to my team to assure the success of this endeavor.

We landed the Kinkos contract, and I got down to running a business. But since this was a temporary contract only until the new owners took over, I become a human sponge again, soaking up all the learning I could, and at the same time working to land a permanent contract to sustain the vision of Precious Time-Hard lessons are learned; the hardest is understanding that while amazing people of great integrity like Cynthia and Paul exist in this world, so do less amazing people of much less integrity. The transitional period ended as did my partnership with my team of childcare experts. Once again I was dancing in the unknown. Only this time, I was dancing with more experience behind me and more confidence in myself. While I'm seeing obstacles in front of me, none of them seem insurmountable.

Then a vendor called with word about a company that had two contracts with major a hospital network that was selling their business. By the time I finished my conversation with them, I had convinced them to consider me as a buyer. I didn't know how I would pay for it, but having danced this dance once, I'd built a list of investors. I had to put aside my fear of "No" to muster the courage to call them. Focusing on the next "Yes", I made a direct "ask" for partnership. It was all moving fast, but deep inside I knew it was going to happen, this contract was going to be mine, this vision of Precious Time was going to be reality.

I didn't have time to engage in even one negative thought. My life was all about making a bold clear request. With an investor ready to go, I purchased the company and its two hospital contracts!

Celebrations!

We signed off on the money with the investors! More celebrations… Until they informed me that they wanted to have majority control on how to run the Precious Time Center. Their vision of how to run it went against mine, and I knew I couldn't compromise the integrity of Precious Time for any amount of money. I called the deal off.

Back I went to the company to figure out a different way to pay them, back into the unknown.

What was on my side? The HR department at the hospital who wanted their childcare center up and running for their employees. As I was trying to complete the deal with the selling company, I located a childcare center near the hospital and proposed to the hospital to allow me to purchase an existing center vs. building a new one which would take much longer. With a mixture of hope and desperation, I met the center owner, Jean Copeland, and managed to get her to consider selling her business to me.

The 11th hour came and it was not easy. My mom passed away, I moved back in with my father, and the company needed their money. But in all this drama and activity, I became aware of the worst-case-scenario, and was very clear to me. Knowing where I stood with how precious this vision was to my heart, I realized

I had given it my all. In the space of gratitude for the journey to date, I was actually at peace with however this dance turned out.

Then... a last chance for a last option and a new idea came to me: Ask Jean Copeland to "seller finance"!

There are days I remember vividly, the day the bomb fell, the day I became a mother, and this day, the one where I got on a call and with all the honesty and integrity I'd learned was fundamental not just to success but to being a good human being on the planet, I told Jean about my vision. Then I told her my truth – about how I was not willing to compromise on my vision for Precious Time.

She agreed and we moved forward. Jean confided that it was my persistence and my passionate belief in my vision that swayed her to my camp. Precious Time was happening! This Dance of the Unknown was complete... except that I knew it wasn't really. I knew it was one step that would be followed by many steps into the unknown.

I do know now that for all the unknowns yet for me to conquer, I have a foundation of "knowns" to support me. "Knowns" of staying true to myself, being authentic with my vision, not to compromise, trust my intuition, being willing to do everything that it takes regardless of how I feel, being in the space of gratitude for what is in my life, creativity is to follow.

If I were to put my message in a phrase, it would be "Perspective Leading to Gratitude". In any challenging situation filled with fear of the unknown, I have discovered two ways of dealing with it. Both requiring me to try on different perspectives like different colored lens sunglasses. As you know if you put on a yellow sunglasses, you will see everything in yellow and so forth.

One perspective is by taking a moment and looking into my past of life and death experiences, I get present to how lucky I am to be alive and able to have THIS challenging moment, and that follows by the space of gratitude. Space of gratitude is being in the highest vibration that makes me feel a shift, uplifting my spirit and empowering me to deal with the challenge in complete ease and trust that this challenge will work out.

One other perspective is to draw from other people's challenging experiences. I see myself as one lucky human being filled with gratitude for all the gifts that I have, from my health, to my beautiful children, to my successful business endeavors.

I'm filled with gratitude for the amazing and powerful, compassionate and wise women – those "knowns" who gave a hand to a young woman entrepreneur, and continue to today: Cynthia Kersey, Jean Copeland and Dianna Loomans. I'm filled with love for my incredible daughters, those two "knowns" who bring their joy, and their passion and their love into every experience we share; the only thing that's bigger than their smiles are their hearts. Finally there is my wonderful partner whose star is aligned to mine and his wisdom.

A footnote to this story is that Cynthia Kersey found a higher and bigger calling and became the CEO and founder of the Unstoppable Foundation that gives tens of thousands of children and their families access to health, education, clean water, housing and self-sustaining income opportunities. I became involved in the Unstoppable Foundation and I am proud to make it part of my giving back to Cynthia and to the world at large.

Elly Molina

Amazon Bestselling author, Elly Molina, is an international intuitive and visionary. She is the founder of psi-kids.com, where children and adults, learn to develop, trust and utilize their intuitive abilities.

Elly has been a lifelong educator. Together with a group of dedicated parents, she co-founded a private school and tailored a Mindfulness Program to meet the specific needs of the school. She works as a psychic and intuitive consultant. She has appeared on FOX, ABC, NBC, CBS, and in the New York Times. Elly's new book, *Children Who Know How to Know*, with Black Opal Publishing was released in March 2017.

For over thirty eight years, she has been instructing children and adults how to develop intuition through techniques which develop and enhance compassion and emotional maturity. She gently instructs children to love, honor, value and respect themselves and others. She teaches parents and children the importance of speaking responsibly and choosing words consciously, always guided by the power of intuition.

Elly is also the author of *Annabelle and the Domino*, an illustrated children's book.

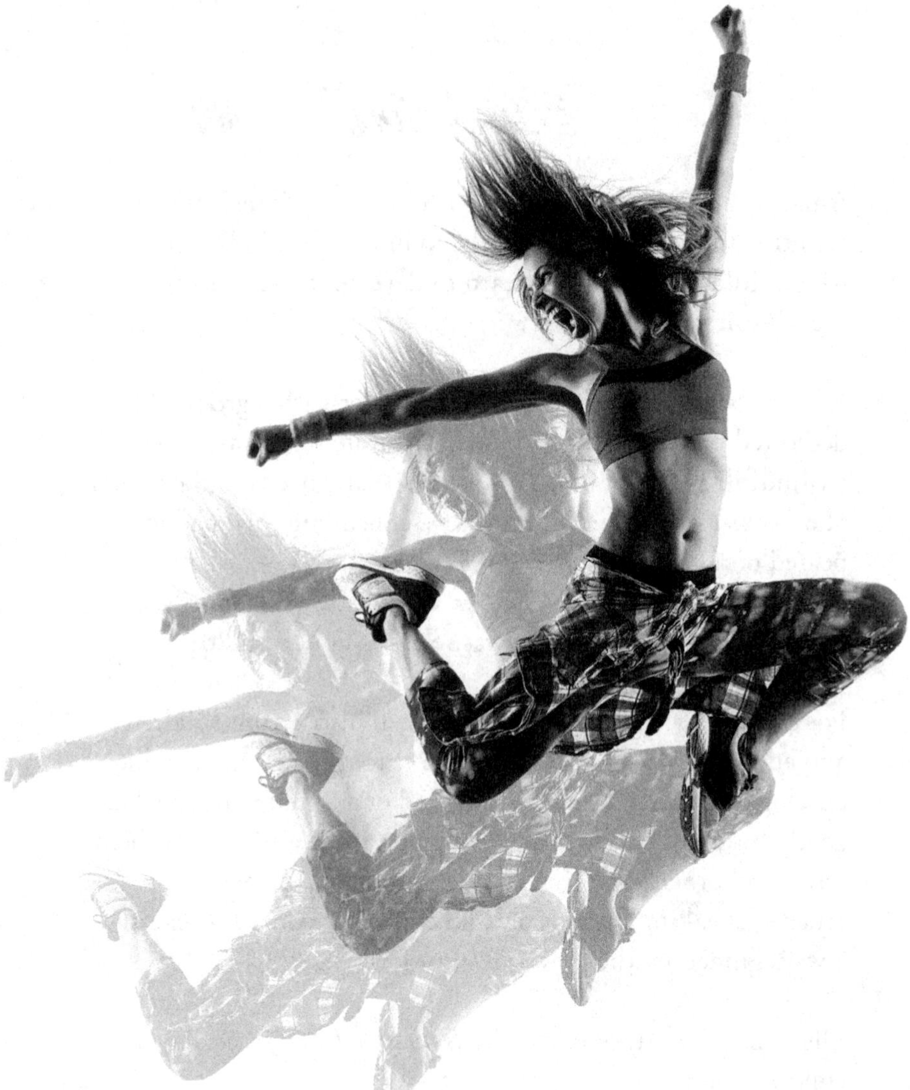

Chapter Nine

REDEFINING COURAGE

By Elly Molina

I've heard it said that many of us know our paths from the time we are children, then spend our lives working to get "home". My pre-school days summed up my entire professional life. I begged my parents for a fortune teller costume which I wore on my first Halloween. I taught geography to stuffed animals, and I packed a suitcase at bedtime each night pretending I would travel around the world and write stories!

I lived sequentially, starting with school, college, graduate school, marriage, children and career. I taught Middle School English, replacing stuffed animals with sixth and seventh graders, while raising my children. Being highly intuitive and psychic, hence the fortune teller costume, turned out to be more challenging. I couldn't help myself from "seeing things" and diligently worked at ignoring the voices and disregarding my intuition. I distracted myself with other people's problems, incompatible relationships and friendships and moved through life that way.

Looking back, I see how I lacked relatable guidance. My parents did their best, yet I struggled relating to them. I created a life that fit me like a small, ugly, itchy sweater, with sleeves and torso too short and uncomfortable. My friends helped pull and stretch the sweater to fit, but being too frightened and trying too hard to please, I refused to take it off. I lacked the courage and self-confidence to pull it off and declare, "This sweater isn't mine and I refuse to wear it."

Webster defines courage as the ability to do something that frightens one. It's synonymous with bravery, audacity, boldness, valor and fearlessness.

At some point, I courageously discarded the terribly worn, frazzled and ill-fitting sweater.

I once believed having courage meant being able to walk into a new experience, despite fear. People have often told me how courageous they see me as.

As a young adult, I moved to a foreign country for five years, where l studied at a university, worked and created both a romantic and social life. That took the kind of courage Merriam Webster defined.

When I travelled to Iran, right before the Revolution, I saw myself as courageous. Not many women were heading in that direction at the time. I wanted experiences and memories.

Later, I felt courageous when I married a man from a different background, taught a new class, a new grade or a new subject. Courageously I opened the first aromatherapy shop back in the day when aromatherapy was in embryonic form in the United States, and hung my "psychic" sign in the store window.

My list of courageous experiences was long. One might look at my life and say, "Wow, you did a lot of dumb things", but that's all perspective isn't it, and what's good for the goose may not be good for the gander.

After twenty-five years of service in the New York Public School system, I needed something more meaningful and drastic. I refused to replace one Long Island suburb for another. Even my friend, Beth, asked, "Why move from one ditch to another?" My colleague, Lorraine's response to my marrying a second time was, "Why divorce, when you're only exchanging a man in a brown suit for a man in a blue suit?" Those comments strengthened my resolve. My next move would be epic!

The adventure began following my second divorce. At a dinner at a friend's house in Colorado I met Pam and Mark. Mark passionately described the beauty of the Pacific Northwest. "Elly, if you're looking for adventure, Washington State is the final frontier, unless you go to Alaska!

I listened in rapt awe. Mark's stories ignited my childhood's romanticized love of the unknown wilderness. He brought back memories of the excitement that stirred within me when my mother read Jack London's *Call of the Wild* to me as a child. The more Mark spoke of America's last frontier, the more I yearned to go. I longed to visit Seattle, where poor Buck was sold, before going to Alaska.

Moving to a remote part of Washington State would be a drastic lifestyle change. My family and I sat at the kitchen table as I shared my Denver experiences.

"We're moving to Washington State!" I declared to all of them.

"Bist voll verrueckt", said my mother. Translated that means: You're crazy!

My two older sons laughed in disbelief, and my youngest son, ten at the time, looked at me and asked, "When are we leaving?"

"When are we leaving?" I repeated out loud, for the benefit of true comprehension and letting this sink in.

I've thought about that moment many times since then. It seemed as if the Universe was giving me a sign to go. I was eligible for twenty-five-years' service in the NYC Public School System's early retirement program, my son would be entering his first year of Middle School and my car's lease would be up all at the same time! Hmmm... Summer, 2008 would be the perfect time to head West!

I believe when things align with our highest good and we intuitively know it's the right choice, events move with velocity and the Universe opens for us.

In March of 2008, I sold my home in three hours to a couple who wouldn't be ready to move in till the end of June. Perfect timing! My son would finish 5th Grade. I would complete my final year as a Language Arts Middle School teacher. My other sons were old enough to live on their own and the move was scheduled for June, 2008.

On June 30th, 2008, my youngest son and I arrived in Washington State. As we pulled into the driveway of our new very rural home, my son climbed out of the new Cadillac Escalade we had rented at Sea-Tac International airport in Seattle. "Mom! You're not going to believe this," he cried, "But there's a peacock in the neighbor's driveway!"

Sure, I thought. I had become accustomed to my son's story-telling, his imagination and his jokes that went beyond the expected capabilities of your average middle schooler. "Okaaaay", I replied, drawing out the last syllable to let him know I wasn't quite buying into his story.

"No, really Mom," he insisted. "Come here, quickly."

When I came around the other side of the car, sure enough, the peacock, later introduced as the neighborhood mascot, Fred, appeared and revealed his fine plumage in either welcome or stay away from my territory behavior.

Wow, he's beautiful, I thought. I remember this overwhelming feeling of ecstasy for having followed my desire for adventure and the unknown.

The move to Rainier, Washington, was one of the most adventurous undertakings I had done since my son's birth. His life was fairly routine: school, video gaming, sports, homework, shower, eat and sleep. It appeared I had a talent for the outrageous and until now I had kept my youngest son protected from participating in my adventures.

For many years, one of my favorite quotes was: "Du fragst mich, Arthur, was soll ich tun und ich sage, Lebe wild und gefährlich". "You ask me Arthur, what should I do, and I say, Live wild and dangerously".

It was a quote I had abandoned after I married.

At that moment, the peacock let out a very shrill noise and I recall walking to the back of the Escalade to remove my three very heavy bags of luggage.

"Well, here we are," I told myself. I looked at the small yellow, one-level house. My thoughts returned to the home we had left only a few hours ago. I replaced the beautiful three story white colonial home, suburban lawns, apple trees, great patio furniture and expensive cars parked in the driveways with this tiny, yellow ranch!

I remember my son's enthusiasm when he saw a wood burning stove for the first time. "Wow, this place has a wood burning stove. Can we use it now?

"It's 90 degrees outside," I replied. "Wood burning stoves are used to keep the home warm. We'll use it when the weather gets colder."

His excitement and pure joy confirmed we had made the right choice.

With each day both our passions for the Pacific Northwest grew, despite missing my two sons, friends and colleagues.

That September, my son began his next level of education. The small private school, tucked away from any trace of urban life, was located on ten acres and nestled amongst 100-year-old Douglas firs. It was an educational paradise. I ended up teaching there. As part of the curriculum we introduced the children to elementary neuroscience, psi- activities, and I spent a good chunk of time teaching children to think outside of the box. We also taught telepathy, remote viewing, blind folded archery and telekinesis!

One afternoon, one of the first graders rushed into class. "Excuse me, Miss Elly." (That's how everyone referred to me.) He was out of breath. "Miss D. wants to let you know, Sarah just moved a domino with her mind!"

Yes, it was true. We had been working on telepathy and telekinesis. Telepathic experiences were the norm. Telekinesis! This was a first!

"I want to share D's story," I told my son one evening.

The event, among others, inspired me to write a children's book in one of my journals. I thought about it a lot and believed it would make an extraordinary book for children and their parents. I dreamed about it. I became obsessed with it and finally just put the journal in a desk drawer and distracted myself by building a house!

In 2009, I hired a local contractor and built a new home on five acres of land overlooking Mt. Rainier.

The phone rang one afternoon. "Mom, I want to move out," my middle son said. "I want to join you and Tony. I need a change. I can't do this anymore." He was college educated and jobless after the events of 2008.

My son moved from New York to join us and help construct the house. I was happy. I now had two of my three sons with me in Washington. I knew my eldest son's calling was to remain in New York. He had a successful career and nice lifestyle.

On February, 10th, 2010, we moved into our newly constructed home. I loved its design. The architect and I designed the great room as a hexagon and the bedrooms were off to the sides. An aerial shot of the house confirmed it looked like a spaceship awaiting take off, totally befitting and honoring the folklore of the lenticular clouds appearing on the horizon over Mt. Rainier.

"Look at the clouds", I said to both of my sons, as we sat on the porch one evening. "You know, it's rumored by some of the locals, these huge lenticular clouds conceal UFOs hovering over the top of the volcano." The locals believe the UFOs chose Mt. Rainier because Ft. Lewis, one of the largest Army bases, was located nearby. The aliens could watch the military and vice versa.

Whether it was my story or not, my middle son decided this was the time to tell me he was moving back East. With the house completed, he felt his purpose in Washington had been fulfilled and departed a few weeks later.

Not long thereafter, I sat outside the wraparound deck, looking at the lenticular clouds again, talking to Margaret, a new friend. The mountain was out that day. It's what we say when Mt. Rainier is visible through the clouds. It's not visible all that often, leaving many tourists unaware of its spectacular and spellbinding beauty.

"Well, what's next?" she asked.

"I want to write and publish a children's book and I have no clue where to begin," I responded.

I realized I was afraid to talk about it. I was afraid to send the manuscript to an editor. I was afraid to seek out an agent or a publisher.

Here is where I learned to redefine courage!

It was easy for me to pack up my family, sell my house, move 2,400 miles across the country, build a new house and create a new life with new friends. Yet, I had brain freeze when I envisioned putting myself out there to look for an editor, agent and publisher. I've walked across a bed of burning hot coals, fearlessly and here I was frozen!

Margaret continued, "Elly, imagine your life five years from now. You'll be five years older, your sons will be five years older, and your life will probably be similar to what it is now. Your book will still be a dream in your desk drawer. You may have regret. You may have a longing to still get it out there."

"Now, imagine your life five years from now. You submitted your book to a publisher and it was accepted. Your book is out there and people can purchase it. Parents are reading it to their children and the children are excited about it."

"How do you feel now?"

Have you ever had that moment of such presence, that you know while it's happening it's a turning point in your life? That conversation was the turning point.

Jack London's *Call of The Wild*, didn't just create a love of the wilderness in me; it also instilled my desire to write. Have you ever felt something so deep in your heart it hurt not to act on it? That was writing for me. For most of my life, I had been afraid to admit that, but sitting there with Margaret I had an "ah-ha" moment. A satori. I had been "doing" courage. I could easily go to new places, partake on new adventures, start new jobs, make new friendships, etc. That form of courage involved doing courage. It wasn't raw and I never felt truly vulnerable.

Publishing my first book took a very different kind of courage. It took courage to listen to my soul and go where it wanted me to go. It was the little seed within me that wanted to grow and I was too frightened to nurture it.

Writing and publicly revealing myself equaled the type of courage my Viking ancestors showed when they set sail for the first time across the dangerous and unpredictable North Sea. Any person who has ever left a job in the corporate world to pursue the calling of their Soul, can probably relate. It takes a special type of courage to follow one's dreams or Soul's calling.

If someone asks me now, "What was the most courageous thing you've ever done?" Without hesitation, my response is, "Writing and publishing my first book, *Annabelle and the Domino*."

I had more fear around this book than when I found myself lost in the woods for many hours, traveled and lived overseas or gave birth three times! But I let go of that fear and did it!

Listening to our Soul's calling requires a different form of courage. It also requires a connection to one's Self.

Since my first book's publication, I've published another book, which became an Amazon best-seller, and I've been writing nonstop for various publications. I am now working on a Young Adult Fiction.

I've learned to listen to my Self/ Soul/ Heart. I've learned to ask it questions and listen for answers. I've learned to trust the answers I receive, even when I think they're supposed to be different. I've learned a new courage.

This courage is trust and faith. It's knowing and trusting that underneath me a safety net exists and no matter what the day looks like, I am always safe.

It takes a very different form of courage to leave the security of a 9-5 steady income life and follow the calling. Since living this way, my life has become more "magical". It has begun to feel more in sync with who I am and why I'm here. I even sleep better at night and no longer stress about the mundane and controlling the illusion.

Oprah says, "There is a supreme moment of destiny calling in our life." If that's the case, and you've heard destiny calling and pulling at your soul, all I can say is, follow.

"Death is not the greatest loss in life. The greatest loss is what dies inside while still alive. Never surrender."
    –Tupac Shakur

Thomas E. Ziemann

Thomas E. Ziemann is a Motivational Keynote speaker who has been featured and interviewed nationally by some of the nation's best internet talk show hosts. Tom delivers uplifting lectures on a diverse catalog of subject matters including: Relationships, Life Purpose, Anger Management, Passion for Living, Sales and Marketing Strategies and Meditation 101. Tom is a published author who has written two books. His first: *The Department of Zenitation; A layman's guide to making spirituality work in Real Life.* His 2nd: *Taming the Anger Dragon; From Pissed off to Peaceful* is due out in late 2017.

Tom's a spiritual researcher with over thirty six years of meditation practice and hosts public and private Satsang's. He offers "Life Purpose, Anger Management, Meditation and Sculpting Classes". He has worked with, mentored, life coached and consulted privately with a myriad of people of all ages with diverse backgrounds.

Tom is the Regional Sales Manager and National Sales Trainer for TechnaGlass. He's an honorably discharged Navy Veteran, married to his best friend and cares for their nine cats. He lives near Portland, Oregon.

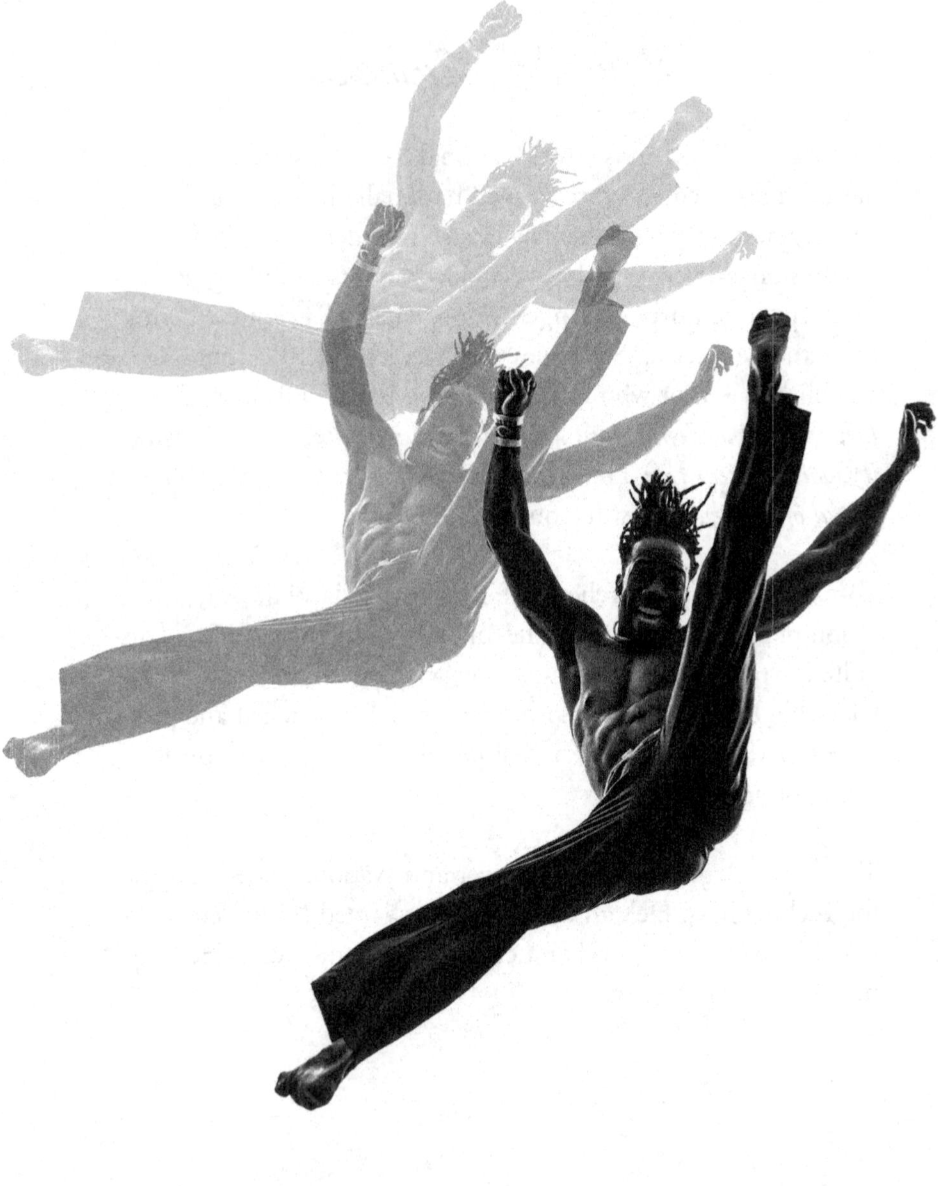

Chapter Ten

DANCING THROUGH THE TSUNAMI

By Thomas E. Ziemann

As I looking back at some fifty-five years I've lived upon this big, blue beautiful marble in space, it's remarkable to reflect on where I've been as where I am now. Had you known me in my youth, you would have seen a disheveled, wimpy, scared, black-eyed and bruised, unconfident, small-stature boy who perfumed the putrid stench of urine well into his early teens. I was the clumsy dork that everyone incessantly teased, picked on and ridiculed – that shy kid you loved to hate and beat the crap out of because it somehow made you feel superior. I was a dour boy whose unrequited love of his parents created a lifelong angst replete with fiery rage from the uncontrolled "Anger Dragon" within that followed me into middle age.

That deep seeded anger left a wake of painful, loveless, tarnished relationships, a broken marriage and premature graying hair. The physical and emotional abuse inflicted by my parents had far reaching ramifications as well as deleterious effects.

Yeah, sadly that was me. As bad as my childhood had been, I hated who I had become as an adult – a self-loathing, sanctimonious, perfectionistic, pompous ass.

I get the question from time to time, "Tom, what the hell happened to you... from that timid little dormouse you used to be to an Enthusiastic, Motivational Speaker and Hope Broker? What I will share in this brief chapter may not work for everyone; however it did work for me.

After graduating high school back in 1981, I met an enlightened man who changed my life. His name was Johnny Norman, a guidance counselor for the Chicago Public Schools as well as an accomplished Taoist Master. He never judged me; rather he graciously offered to take me under his loving tutelage. What made his teachings different from most other Martial Art schools was that he concluded every class with a different type of meditation every time. He knew literally hundreds of them. I was blessed to study under this incredible man for well over a year before joining the Navy. While Kung Fu helped my confidence, it was the meditation techniques which helped me focus my monkey mind and to find some inner peace.

To a point. The anger I was holding onto towards my parents darkly colored every other area of my life. I found myself to be an Anger-Holic. A perfectionistic A'hole. A total judgmental bastard. All for what? Why?

When I hit fifty, many of the answers seemed blatantly obvious to me. What allowed me to finally face my inner demons were two things. First, the Big F: Forgiveness. Until I came to terms with the fact that my parents did the best they could within the awareness they had, my life would never change. A huge spiritual weight was lifted of my chest once I let go of all the self-pity I was harboring.

Secondly, I was finally able to see myself clearly in an unflattering light. The truth can be painful, yet it's equally liberating.

Once I was emotionally and spiritually mature enough to accept myself as I was, it allowed the healing process to commence. For the first time in my life I was able to simply admit how screwed up I was. I took ownership of my past mistakes and made a vow to myself to change. To make right the wrongs I had done where possible and give back.

Both of my books, *The Department of Zenitation* and *Taming the Anger Dragon,* delve quite deeply into the processes which share more intimate details than time allows here. While there are no perfect prescriptions defining what makes one happy and how to heal oneself, I will share a few things I found invaluable along my path.

The healing began with an evaluation and deep examination of my beliefs. This included all aspects of my make-up – mental, emotional, spiritual, philosophical, political and so on. This was carried out with a series of reflective questions. Why did I believe what I believed? How did I come to these preconceived notions? Were they still valuable to me? Had I grown beyond these preconceived ideas? Did they still have merit? Had I delved deep enough into their importance?

Once I felt I had a good grasp of my beliefs, it allowed me to go deeper. Who am I? Why am I here? Each question took me deeper, an existential quest so to speak. This line of questioning begged an honest answer to this important question: What was my life purpose? Immediately I knew that mine was to help others define their own purpose. What's yours? Once you can answer that, I promise you that your life will change provided you heed your inner calling.

When you are in touch with your core being, your answer will become apparent. You will have a choice; that point on your path; to go for your dream or not. Don't worry what others will think about yours, that's not important. What does matter is that you take the time to contemplate why you are here. Don't worry how you will accomplish your goal. Leave that to a higher power. Remember that there is nothing worthwhile for free in life. One must work to make things happen.

You will know how important what you say is your life purpose by the amount of time you spend daily thinking about it and working towards its fruition.

Once I defined my life purpose, it allowed a number of things to really sink in. First it helped me know myself deeper than ever before. It allowed me to love myself as I hadn't previously experienced. What an amazing peaceful feeling! I speak not of a narcissistic love, but of an acceptance of all my good parts as well as my faults. No judging, just acknowledging them. This is a freeing exercise which I whole heartily recommend you doing.

You cannot love another fully without first loving yourself. Understanding one's strength and weakness is invaluable as it shows us where to focus our attention. Using one's gifts to work on areas where we fall short is nothing less than magical. Being the right person will make finding the one a much easier task. I realize this may all be a lot to take on all at once, that's not the purpose. Don't try to conquer everything you're unhappy with at once. Simply choose your battles as they come. Big changes and rewards come with time and daily focus on the problem. Taking time daily to add to your understanding of things will help immensely in rounding out one's life.

I have a thirst for knowledge, an unquenchable desire to know something about everything. Not to be an expert on every subject, simply wise enough to be able to ask intelligent questions.

Real wisdom is grown that way.

In my earlier years, I took things too personally. It ruined many burgeoning relationships. Not taking myself too seriously has been a blessing. As the great American Buddhist teacher Pema Chodron often says, "Lighten up on yourself."

We generally receive the love that we believe we deserve, so open your heart to all possibilities.

Of course, what we all seek is true happiness. I could devote an entire book to this one. Happiness is not about what happens to us; rather, it's how we choose to respond to what happens to us. Happiness is not about having what you want; it's about wanting what you already have. It is not determined by what's happening around you, but rather what's happening inside of you. One secret to happiness is to do what you like; the reward of a successful life is truly liking what you do. It takes one area of one's life to be off kilter to play emotional havoc. Maslow spoke in great depth about this fact in his hierarchy of needs. The best definition of real happiness I've ever heard is; someone to love, something to do and something to look forward to. Powerful wisdom indeed.

Let's break this parable down. "Someone to love" can also be equated to something one loves. For our discussion I will focus on the relationship aspect. Relationships, good or bad, can have a profound effect on one's emotional being. Having a significant other who you love is paramount to a long fruitful relationship. They can add many years of health as well. Believing you are worthy of having such a relationship is only part of the equation. Once you get that dream partner is when the work begins.

Sadly, many people have chosen to stay in lackluster relationships as opposed to being alone. They are dying a slow spiritual death by doing so.

No one can tell you how to define a meaningful relationship. By discovering who you are, you will gravitate to what you desire and what will create greater joy in your life. As I've discussed in *Taming the Anger Dragon*, knowing your and your partner's "joy triggers" will make finding and keeping a relationship blossoming a snap. Relationships are never easy and good ones are incredibly fulfilling. Timing plays a huge role in this so keep an open heart. Choosing the right partner is critical.

What's the secret to creating a lasting magical relationship? Seek to be in a relationship where both partners never stop trying. Mutual respect is the key. Act loving, enthusiastic and be in the moment when you're with people. Put that cell phone down when having a conversation. Use reflective listening to really understand what your partner means and their needs.

The perfection trap has doomed many relationships. Don't seek a perfect person; they don't exist. Instead cultivate a relationship with someone who's perfect for you, someone who accepts you with all your faults, imperfections and visa-versa. The starting point for this is with you, not with your partner. If you are dissatisfied with yourself, I can promise you that you will never find a person who can truly and fully satisfy you.

Here's a question to ponder: What's more important in a relationship, to be loved or respected? Respected of course. Why is that true? That's because you can love someone and not respect them. However, if you respect the other, love is the byproduct.

We've discussed the relationship portion of the three legs of happiness. Now let's discuss the "something to do" aspect. The great neurologist and psychiatrist Viktor Frankl document-ed that people who have a reason to live generally do despite unfathomable obstacles. His message is simple; know what you love to do. One's career can supply much happiness and self fulfilment as doing the thing that makes your heart sing. How do you know what you love doing?

A great exercise is creating your bucket list. Simply stated, your list is nothing more than a specific inventory of every dream you've ever had. The key point is to not judge them. Allow your beautiful mind to flow. Let your deeply hidden wants and aspirations translate into words on paper. One's latent talents can be cultivated and create incredible joy in one's later life. Be creative! Don't let the lack of money or means to be a barrier on your list. As it's been said, the universe conspires to make your dreams come true if you know what they are. Want them with all your heart. Burning desire combined with definiteness of purpose, specificity and action make dreams become reality.

Having a goal to reach has allowed people from all walks of life to live longer, more fulfilling lives. If they could just make it to one more Christmas, to see their children get married, to see the birth of their grandchildren. The list goes on and on. Ironically a good number of the signers of the Declaration of Independence all died on July 4th, Coincidence? I think not. It's my belief they all had a reason to go on. What do you look forward to?

We come now to the last part of this chapter. To make the case for how I got here from where I came from can be rephrased as "How I learned to dance through the Tsunami".

I can't make one single argument identifying one incident that was the reason for setting me on my path. Certainly there were many catalysts. As I said earlier, forgiveness is a true healer. I don't do it for the one who wronged me; I do it to give myself inner peace.

I've learned far more from my failures than my successes. I've also had the good fortune to be able to learn vicariously from others. In other words I didn't have to experience what they did to glean the lesson or the hurt they endured.

"Taming my Anger Dragon", using anger and my pain for fuel was a necessary part in breaking my anger cycle and addiction. Coming to the realization I was miserable in my life gave me the courage to face my inner demons.

Taking calculated risks has added to my life tenfold. In no way could I have accomplished anything without risking.

Music has been a soothing, life altering tonic. I listen to music daily to help calm the inner beast known as anxiety.

Daily meditation has also been a lifesaving, sanity activity. Teaching meditation classes has made me a far better student. Learning proper breathing techniques has literally saved my health.

Making peace with past was a big part of the healing I required. Sharing my vulnerabilities on the written page has helped me enormously. In doing so, I realized there are many others out there who also carry much of the same pain and fear I did. They can gain helpful insights by reading my plight without having to endure the same.

Being able to see myself in an unflattering light was the key part in coming to terms with my short comings, thereby accepting myself as I was and using my faults as a starting place for change. Taking the time to know myself completely was a tremendous gift to myself.

Realizing life isn't fair helped me to become self-sufficient and strive to accept tragedies easier. Bad things happen to everyone. I am not being singled out by a vengeful God.

In life, there is no free ride. When I want more, I must work smarter and/or harder to obtain my dreams and desires.

Using gratitude as a part of my everyday existence changed my life immediately for the better. Taking time daily to appreciate where I am, how truly blessed I am, what gifts I have, who is in my life and all the gifts bestowed upon me right this second.

Practicing random daily acts of kindness to people who can never repay me has changed my life immeasurably.

Becoming my own best friend helped me create amazing friendships around the world, some stemming over forty years!

To be able to ask others for help was a biggie for me. As the old Chinese adage says: "He who goes through life with a clenched fist receives nothing."

Learning to delay immediate gratification has been a heaven sent, financially freeing realization.

Being able to share my deepest feelings with my wife and close friends without fear of having them judge me has been a miraculous experience.

Learning to communicate effectively has certainly reaped positive benefits. While expressing myself clearly is certainly important, learning to listen without trying to figure out what the other was saying before they finished was a big one for me.

To give honest praise and appreciation to the people and employees in my life has been key to my success.

Writing down my goals has allowed me to live a fuller life than I ever believed possible.

Giving something back daily (even a kind word) may be the greatest gift to myself I've ever received.

Helping charities and non-profits raise donations has given me a deep sense of accomplishment and a self-satisfaction that I only dreamt about in my early years.

Seeing the joy my sculptures create in the eyes of the receiver and onlookers has filled me with a great sense of joy.

Allowing the love that I have desperately sought my entire life to flow to me, rather than chasing it allowed me to give more love back than I ever believed possible.

Knowing and working daily towards my life purpose has given me inner peace. Helping others identify theirs has been beyond gratifying.

Spending time daily with all nine of my wonderful cats has added many years of happiness to my life.

Working in my garden and yard has created joy and satisfaction that come from seeing one's effort pay off.

Home entertaining, cooking for my friends and family has been one of the greatest gifts I have ever given myself. Generosity begets the same.

Developing the passion deep within has pushed me to greater height's than I believed I was capable of.

Keeping true to my deepest beliefs such as "The Truth is one and the paths are many" has helped me keep an open mind unhampered by prejudice and judgment.

Writing several books has been life changing to say the least. It helped develop my confidence and hopefully creates joy for my readers.

Public speaking has given me the deep satisfaction of helping others find their own way. Becoming a "Hope Broker" has added an indescribable joy which eluded me most of my life.

Finding the woman of my dreams late in life showed me that amazing things come to those who never give up hope. By becoming the person I sought rather than just searching for her has given me the loving marriage I had always desired.

I wish each and every one of you the inner peace you are seeking.

Dr. Nelly Farnoody-Zahiri

Dr. Nelly Farnoody-Zahiri is a keynote speaker and a world-renowned clinical psychologist who specializes in working with children and families. Her areas of expertise are in Mindfulness, Eastern and Western Psychology Integration, School Counseling, Educational Counseling, Cross-Cultural Psychology, Attachment Parenting, Pre and Post Divorce Counseling, PeaceLearning Partnership, Partnership Counseling, and Conscious and PeaceLearning Parenting. She's the author and founder of the International Center For Peace Learning and the popular parenting show on Satellite TV and YouTube *MomTalk Dr. Nelly.*

Dr. Nelly has been in private practice in the Los Angeles area for over ten years, and she's an active member of The American Psychological Association. She has also produced and hosted educational and psychological events and programs in the U.S.A and Internationally.

Dr. Nelly has an upcoming book in the field of Peace Psychology, Childhood Development, Character, Parenting, Leadership, and Peace Learning Living. Her Mission for MomTalk is to raise awareness regarding Mental Health, Conscious Parenting and Mindfulness.

Dr. Nelly lives with her husband and three children in Los Angeles, and she enjoys small gatherings and cooking international foods, praying and meditation, yoga, self-compassion practices, hiking, skiing, going for walks on the beach, soul cycling, drumming, Zumba, dancing and listening to World Music.

Chapter Eleven

MOTHERHOOD AWAKENING INTO THE UNKNOWN

By Nelly Farnoody-Zahiri, Ph. D.

As a voyager, traveling throughout life I have experienced circumstances where I was pushed way beyond my comfort and peace zone into mystery... into the unknown space, where I could explore and experience curiously about life and seek to understand and unfold the mysterious relationship between Peace, Love and Conflict. This "Golden PeaceLearning Triangle" has guided me to make wiser choices in life and living.

The early years of my life here in the U.S., where I grew up in the 70's during "The Peace Movement", were happy days. My parents, who were Graduate Students and Iranian, were studying to take part of the Leadership in the Westernization of the Iranian Educational Systems. When I was six, we moved back to Iran, and my entire world was turned upside down. Not only didn't I speak the language (Farsi), the Eastern-Western cultural clashes created a strong enough cultural divide to lead me to spend my entire life attempting to integrate Eastern-Western Living, Psychologies, PeaceLearning Parenting, Conscious Parenting, as well as helping families in conflict. I spent my school years seeking how to heal my own wounds, and how to support others in healing theirs.

By the way, PeaceLearning is a verb I created to describe this transformational and healing process and work. It is a conscious intent to unfold the relationship between peace, conflict and unconditional love. It's a process of learning and integrating those understandings and personal experiences around peace, conflict and love into your everyday life. In every moment, there are aspects of all three occurring simultaneously and the process is to learn to integrate and create balance. PeaceLearning is what helps one to create a sense of Well-Being, existing and living in this constant flux of the three.

My life took another turn when our family fled Iran due to the 1979 Iranian Revolution. We moved back to the United States, and this time the move and cultural divide impacted my growth and transition into high school, college and womanhood.

Surrounded by my Iranian-American peers during my college years, I almost followed them into our Community's preferred professions: Dentistry, Medicine, Engineering or Law! As immigrant families, we were expected to choose one of those fields for success.

I began to experience some pressure and anxiety about my chosen path when I decided to take a summer break, a pause to self-reflect, travel, explore freely, seek and find my calling!

After some self-analysis and self-exploration, I decided to become a scientist-practitioner in understanding Human Development, Healing Trauma and Cultivation of Well-Being. I studied Psychology and ultimately became a Clinical Psychologist, focusing on family and children. I spent my career guiding families in building strong relationships, teaching parenting classes and counseling children how to better cope with their life stressors. The irony was that I wasn't a parent yet.

My husband and I had waited to have children until we were older and settled in our professions. When we decided to start a family, we expected one child – and this is where God's sense of humor came into play.

I imagine that God thought, *"Okay, you'd love to be a mom? You want to be a parent. Here you go!"* We learned that I was pregnant with twins. This was the beginning of an infinite and beautiful motherhood journey into the unknown! As intense and challenging as it was, it was also amazingly beautiful. It felt as if I were growing on parallel tracks faced with intense love, conflict and challenge. I knew my life would change with the birth of a child and I wasn't necessarily prepared for having two, but at the same time I was witnessing and being with the beauty of life and what it offers us in growth and spirituality.

In the Fall of 2007, I give birth to two beautiful children, our son, Cyrus Christopher, and our daughter, Camellia Noor. I was in AWE, in LOVE, in a daze of exhaustion, exhilaration, joy and fear, all the things a new parent experiences. I recall the moment when I found myself. I experienced a deeper sense of integration and my way to becoming a Mother, a Psychologist and a Wife. I found My PeaceLearning Path!

Any breast-feeding mother knows that experience of feeling like a cow. Yeah, I was a "Peaceful Cow" in bed, pumping. Camellia, our daughter, had colic and she would cry intensely, which made caring for the two of them difficult. We ended up hiring help, which meant dealing with several caregivers. As a new mom, I was managing the help and our wonderful extended family of course. We're a big family so everyone wanted to be involved. I was getting a lot of "advice" on what we needed to do for our daughter's tummy and I was becoming frustrated with the conflicting information from all the caretakers. I was pumping 24/7, not sleeping, feeling not human, and I just had a moment in exhaustion, an epiphany, like I literally saw everything go white and disappear in my head and I thought, *"I'm Okay!"* A pause in time, and an out of body experience to laugh about it; I got happy and peaceful in my head space. I said, "Okay, just take a deep breath, you got this." I told myself to look at everything – just observe – and stay present to the "AS IS!" I was able to observe and be without any judgment.

After a while of just observing without judgment, I felt my inner voice or my inner spirit guiding me, calling me to stay connected to that "PeaceLearning Mindset". I heard the words "just let it go" and "freedom" flowing through me like a mantra. Just let go! My inner maternal intuition told me, "You don't need to be in your head, in your mind, just let it go. Drop it. Look into your children's eyes, do what you do naturally and know you are okay." I repeated the affirmation that I was "okay". The knowledge that "I am" made me feel confident and connected. I felt like nothing else really mattered anymore. The little things that were bothering me before didn't really matter. In that moment, I let go of my obsession with the delusion of control. I was awakened and became aware of my being and felt amazingly peaceful and free.

I became conscious, aware, confident and assertive. I let go of the help, made some changes, improved my communication with others, stayed true to myself and rearranged our whole environment to feel right to the PeaceLearning Relationships. I told myself I was going through this personal experience, this wonderful spiritual awakening and it was time to let go of the need to want to know the unknown and of my obsessional delusion to want to control my children and my family.

I had a lot of empathy and compassion for my family and for the families I had counseled early in my practice. I used to guide and help these families but I was inexperienced and clueless about the organic and hands-on parenting experiences. I was coming from a place of science, and interpersonal neurobiology rather than a place of heart, empathy and compassion. I remember feeling compelled to call back all the parents whom at times I had judged and say to them, "Listen I am sorry. I know how difficult this must be for you." I wanted to show them empathy and compassion. I remember thinking to myself, *"No one should ever be able to teach a parenting class if they're not a parent themselves!"*

Just following that experience, having that awakening, I remember the sense of safety, a sense of belonging, a sense of security and feeling that things were going to be okay by allowing freedom and mindfulness to guide my path. There was no need to map out everything or be obsessed with being in control, now that I was becoming more Mindful and more aware of "Me" and "Me-We" of parenting.

We humans are often opposed to transformation or change because it's a stressful process. Child rearing was very stressful for me. Having two babies of two different genders to bond with, nurse and care for simultaneously was not easy.

Adding to that was the discovery that I was pregnant with our second daughter, our precious Chloe Rose. It was super joyful and beautiful, but also super challenging for a young mother of three! Not to mention my big fancy extended family. I know that as wonderful as that can be, there is always some sort of drama in navigating between all relationships! Our family of five did get a lot of support, but we also had to face multiple conflicts in relationships and the care givers many different

needs, and opinions which made it difficult to hear my own inner voice above all the chatter and drama.

I recall an incident like this, just seconds before going into the delivery room, when my husband invited my sister-in-law to join us. He did ask for my permission in the moment, and of course I said "yes!" because I love my sister-in-law, but I also felt ambivalent about sharing the sacred space and experience of our Twins Birth with someone else. This is one of those co-parenting moments when I had to let go, because of the power of the situation, and embrace the mystery of the PeaceLearning path and honor the push to integrate, accept or reject the "As-is". I found myself in this beautiful place of The Unknown. Thinking that I knew, but needed to open up and be reminded, that there would be much more PeaceLearning Discoveries!

I am a child psychologist with a passion for PeaceLearning Living and Mindfulness. I had all the clinical expertise, experimental expertise, the research background, and of course with mentors like Dan Siegel, Shefali Tsabary, and Jean Piaget, Mary Ainsworth, John Bowlby, and many more, I stood the risk of becoming over-confident. Little did I know how parenting from the inside-out would change my life!

I went into this experience of giving birth and being a parent thinking, "Oh this is going to be fabulous. I am going to have a beautiful motherhood journey, my baby and I will bond and we will all live happily ever after!" Then came the reality of having twins and getting pregnant a year later with our third. The PeaceLearning Path and Journey appeared after that epiphany when I was pushed full force into The Unknown, when I discovered the power in giving up my delusion of control. Yes, I had many expectations about the way it "was going to be" and "The Illusion". What I learned was to open "The Heart" and

"The Soul", to listen to "The Inner Voice" and to take small and simple steps on to this path of PeaceLearning as a Parent, a Mother, as a Wife and as a Clinical Psychologist. I learned to have self-compassion and live with more "Freedom".

In a way, giving birth and becoming a mother was an awakening in the context of a tribal and communal experience. I had to learn to navigate between multiple relationships and multiple needs, feelings and expectations. In my PeaceLearning Core there was much to work through, many thoughts and feelings, many dynamics, my own early years' experiences, and my husband's early years' experiences, the clashing of our cultures sometimes, and our merging of parenting and co-parenting. When you are the parents of multiples and have to endure the attunement, the nursing, the sleepless nights – that's when you realize, you can't plan it, you can't obsess over wanting to know it, you can't control it, you can't be a step ahead of it, you just have to be. My new mantra was "Stay Cool and Let It Go!" You have to be relaxed with the unknown and understand that the control is an illusion. My accepting the unknown and the "As-Is" started me on this this beautiful PeaceLearning Journey.

The unknown space of fear and doubt brought up the fear of rejection and the fear of having hurt the feelings of my family members, when I had to express myself and set new boundaries. During those encounters and communications, I realized that I was not in PeaceLearning, but rather in a place of War-Learning! Every day I was going to war in a conflict zone. I felt like a WarriorMom and it was hard work. I was awakened to new dimensions of my life, myself, my family and my community; shedding the old and allowing a new deeper connection to myself and others. There were many times when I felt remorse, guilt and shame, but there were just as many moments when I experienced tremendous growth and transformation. Surely,

there were times when all I could feel was suffering, my mind-set of "Depressive Realism", "What Have We Done?" But there were more times when I could consciously allow my soul to be nourished, experience self-compassion, growth, transformation and to develop new relationships where things were different and more peaceful!

In any transformational experience, whether it be becoming a parent, losing a parent or spouse, getting married, moving, or changing careers, there are stressful transformational touch points and moments in which you have the opportunity to find a deeper connection to your spirit, to your soul, to your inner voice and your inner guide. It's an opportunity to choose to stay on the path of consciousness or take the wisdom and expand, evolve and ultimately choose a new one.

I started off as being not too self-compassionate towards myself, as a newcomer to the Motherhood Journey. I was not taking enough time to myself to rejuvenate and practice self-care. Often I went through days trying to survive and complete one more touch point. Those were moments when I really needed to slow down and be more present. I had to practice self-compassion and self-care. Now that I've become a more mature and aware PeaceLearning Parent, I'm a huge advocate of cultivating character and self-compassion and self-care. I actively look for the family's integration with compassion, peaceful communication, care and cooperation and its direct relationship to reduced-suffering, and building a well-balanced Happy and Healthy Environment.

When I experienced my awakening, the moment in which everything finally came to a head, I stopped and heard my inner voice and I made choices that have served me well. That was the beginning of my PeaceLearning Living. The cultivation of well-being for my babies, my family, my friends, my community and it all comes from a place of compassion, empathy, a wisdom of knowing that I can't do it all, that I don't need to control or fix it all. I found trust and faith in my own intuition and inner guidance. I started to open up, reach out and ask for help. I expanded my circle of trusted mom-friends and mentors. I became a visionary woman... a PeaceLearning Visionary! I started a twins' parenting group and I knew that I was connecting not just for my own well-being, but also for the well-being of our bigger community. This self-realization and actualization made it a very healing experience, which led to tremendous interpersonal and self-integration in the path to seeking growth, character, peace and well-being. This shared narrative experience made it meaningful, because in a very meaningful way, I was not alone anymore. We had a shared vision, and a path which we had chosen to travel together. That feeling of being connected to others experiencing similar challenges and knowing that we had mysteriously and collectively entered the field of the "Unknown" with the intent of PeaceLearning made it all worthwhile!

Throughout these challenges, I have discovered my strength! I had no idea I was capable of this "WarriorMom" strength. Although at times it was a very emotional experience, it was also very much a spiritual journey. My life was turned upside-down, but maybe sometimes we need those shifts to find our Peace-Learning Core.

My husband and I went from zero to three in three years, and the first three years of our PeaceLearning Parenting experiences had coincided with my turning forty. Talk about an existential crisis. I mean literally within that month of turning forty I had another spiritual awakening, which was not the same thing as my Conscious Parenting Awakening. This time my intuition was leading me to seek the unknown, to let go my attachment to things and that of materialistic value. I was also feeling encouraged to let go my resistance to change and the rigid "Ego", to let go my illusion of attachments, as I experienced an organic separation and individuation which had more of a spiritual quality to it. I started experiencing a deeper relationship with my "Soul", "God", "Spirituality" and "The Unknown".

I realized, if you don't have that type of spiritual connection and relationship and awareness and your intentional focus is not there, you are going to be distracted with all the noises that will keep you from your calling and your purpose in life. I opened myself up to pay attention to the here and now, and became more aware of the big picture, emerging in PeaceLearning Living with presence and not worrying about all the small things in life.

This shift in my consciousness and mindset has made a huge difference in my personal and professional development. I have become a more peaceful human being, and a seeker of truth and happiness. I started my Momtalk TV, and my intentional conversations around PeaceLearning Parenting, Conscious Parenting, Conscious Media, Mindfulness, Well-Being and Wholistic Integration. As a result of being more conscious, I also started having these amazing spiritual encounters and experiences with Spiritual Leaders like His Holiness Dalai Lama, Amma, Patrick McCollum, Deepak Chopra, Dr. Shefali, Oprah, Gary Zukav, Mallika Chopra and many more amazing mentors who have made my life more meaningful as a Super-Soul and PeaceLearning Leader.

Our three warmhearted children have made this journey one of the most profound experiences of my life! I am honored and massively grateful for being their mom. My PeaceLearning and spiritual development continues to thrive, and my willingness to be a little more compassionate with others as well as myself is a mindful daily practice. I have learned to trust and practice my leap of faith often and to be more aware of my inner voice and my ability to dance in the unknown and know that I am beautiful just the way I am. I am warmhearted and appreciate kindness, I am okay with messiness and the chaos in Peace-Learning Living and living with PeaceLearning Intent is my passion and joy.

I know in my heart that I'm a seeker, a lover and a peacemaker. This Motherhood Journey has given me the opportunity to cultivate the peace I yearned for as a child, the peace I desired to give to others by becoming a clinical psychologist and the peace I desired to experience and nurture as a Soul Leader, Daughter, Sister, Wife and Mom.

Take a leap of faith, find your spiritual center, connect within and you too will enjoy this PeaceLearning Journey.

Ronda Renée

Ronda Renée has been called a modern day mystic with "x-ray vision for your soul". Ronda is an international speaker, facilitator, best-selling author and Life Fulfillment and Spiritual Business Mentor. Ronda has the unique ability for making the mystical practical.

Having learned that all the "things" we think will make us happy never quite seem to, Ronda went on an intense inner exploration that led her to discovering her life's work of teaching people how to live, love and work from their Soul.

As the creator of Your Divine Navigation System®, Ronda teaches you how to align with your unique energetic soul signature, your Divine Coordinates®, enabling you to fully embrace your Divine Design and live a life of deep meaning, purpose and satisfaction.

Knowing that true success and fulfillment can only be found by living and working in alignment with your soul, through her Business in Your Soul® program, Ronda helps transformational entrepreneurs and service professionals to identify, design and run their business from their soul so they can make the difference and the money they were meant to. Find out more at DivineNavigation.com.

Chapter Twelve

I MIGHT FALL, BUT I MIGHT FLY!

By Ronda Renée

"Let me fall if I must fall. The me I become will catch me."
—UNKNOWN

I've never been a fan of roller coasters or fast cars. I never had the urge to bungee jump or skydive out of an airplane either. Leaping off cliffs in my life, however, is another story entirely. These, I can't resist. At least that's how it appears, as often as I seem to do it. I step off cliffs like I'm stepping off of a curb. Here I am once again mid-air.

I was asked during an interview awhile back if I had always been a risk taker. The idea of that makes me giggle a bit. I lead a pretty quiet life by most accounts. I prefer ritual and rhythm in my daily life over the drama and chaos that so many others seem to feed on.

I'm less of a risk taker and more of a possibility maker.

The allure of a new vista, the draw of a dream coming true, the possibility of a new reality, the enticement of a vision becoming manifest, pulls me to the edge of the proverbial cliff. If you hang out on the edge of a cliff, looking down at the how far you could fall, you are likely to get scared, almost certain to get dizzy and most will back away from that edge.

I, on the other hand, having tired of having my toes hanging off the edge, am willing to free fall into a new reality – repeatedly. Once again I step off the cliff. I might fall.... but I might FLY!

Some of my most notable leaps have included accelerating my studies in order to graduate from high school at sixteen; moving 3000 miles across country only one month after turning seventeen; choosing to move to Colorado when my daughter was less than a year old only one year after purchasing my first home in Virginia making me a landlord for the first time at age twenty-four; jumping on board with a no-name company in the industry I worked in to open up a new territory in the state of Colorado and going on to be top sales producer for them for over ten years; getting married for the second time having only dated the guy for six months (in case you were wondering, not all my leaps pan out!); ultimately leaving that very lucrative secure six-figure job to start my own coaching and training company. Along the way there were plenty of other less notable "little" leaps.

My most recent leap has actually turned out to be a series of leaps. I gave away, sold or otherwise got rid of close to eighty percent of my possessions, sold the family home where I had raised my kids and saying goodbye to my hometown of twenty-two years. All to set off to start a new life 1,100 miles away in a new state with a new man.

After over two years of a long distance relationship repeatedly traversing the span between our homes, including a couple of stints of part time bi-location living, I had grown weary of the back and forth but not of the relationship. Right about that time he indicated that he was also ready to consider going to the next stage of our relationship and moving in together.

The process of the move started out very promisingly. I got a contract on my house the very first day it was shown. Just what you'd want right? On the other hand, clearing out and closing up a home you have lived in for the majority of eighteen years is no small project. It also was not the kind of project that I could delegate. I was going to have to be the one to do it and it was all consuming!

Luckily as an entrepreneur I have complete command over my calendar. I moved all nonessentials aside, pushed back new projects and got to work on being ready for the closing day a few weeks later.

I was blessed to have a very large wooded lot in the heart of the city. The quiet park like neighborhood is idyllic, something that is almost unheard of nowadays, at least at an affordable price. With a third of an acre lot there was plenty of room to grow. A rare gem indeed!

By many accounts the best room in the house is a sunroom addition that sits elevated in the pine trees with full length windows on three sides. It's most people's favorite room in the house. When I bought the house, the room had seventies shag carpeting, dark brown laminate paneling and an antiquated hot tub sitting in the middle of the room. I removed the hot tub, replaced the paneling with drywall, installed new craftsman style wood paned windows, and put in new flooring. It felt like an oasis sitting amongst the pines!

The potential new owner had plans to expand the house and asked if I had the permit for the sunroom. "No, I don't. It was here when I bought the house," I told my agent. The new owner went to the city to get a copy of the permit only to discover that there wasn't one.

It dawned on me that there was no permit at the city because the property had been in the county when it was built. It was going to take potentially several weeks to get the archived permit.

The day that my moving trailer was delivered, I agreed to allow the new owner to bring his contractor friend and inspect the property before closing with the understanding that things would be in disarray as we would be actively loading up to move out.

In addition to his contractor friend, the new owner was also joined by his two real estate agents. As they toured the property and inspected the addition, I could feel the energy of the group begin to change. Something was wrong. I *could* feel it!

I went inside to share my concerns with my man who was there to help me in the final stages of packing.

"Something's wrong," I said.

"Everything's fine," he insisted. "Don't worry." Of course he was going to be supportive but I knew he was wrong.

Whatever the contractor friend said to the would-be owner spooked him and within hours he had pulled out of the contract just as my proverbial train was ready to pull out of the station. What was I to do? All of the furniture was already packed. The plans had been made. It was like being in midstream and looking back at the shore thinking, "I know I leaped into this water but can't I just go back to shore?"

I am a scrappy one though. I'm used to shifting with the tides. Admittedly, I tend to be the kind of person who leaps and then figures it out on my way down. I found myself once again mid-air not knowing exactly where I'd land, or if I'd fly or simply fall.

This was not going to stop me from moving confidently forward in the direction of my dreams! There was no looking back for me. I had put my stake in the ground and I was going for it. It's a great house and I had a comfortable position in it. I was inconvenienced but I wasn't worried.

When the move was originally discussed, my man and I were going to move into a new place together to start fresh in a space that was "ours". At some point in the process he panicked and asked if we could try staying at his current place. He had thought it through and had lots of remedies in mind for how it could work for us all.

By the time I got "settled" into his current place I had been in some state of packing and moving for a good six weeks. I was exhausted, homesick and very ready to turn my attention fully back to my work.

My guy also worked at home, which meant that there was always something happening on the home front. Added to two busy entrepreneurs was his young adult son whose schedule was unpredictable and whose energy was let's just say more than a bit challenging for my sensitive constitution. As much as he tried, as much as we wanted it to work, it just didn't.

I was already completely untethered. Not being able to work (which is like breathing to me!) made things even worse. I felt less and less like "me" and started to question nearly every choice I had made.

While I may have been tempted to return to Colorado, my

house was already under contract again. I didn't live there anymore. I lived here now. Period. Plus I knew that going "back" was not the answer anyway. The Universe had brought me this far. It must want me here.

It was time for another leap. I was going to have to move out.

I'll never forget the day that I came to that realization. It was a Tuesday and a rare occasion that I was alone in the house. But how much it didn't feel like home was ringing in my ears as loudly as if there was a stereo blasting at full volume. My very next thought was, "I wonder if my former landlord I rented the studio I used to have here has another place for rent." Then I brushed it aside and went on about what I had on my agenda for the day.

By week's end, it was undeniable. I had to go. I was so upset that I was up all night until 5 a.m. on Saturday morning. Around 3 a.m. I got on the computer and hopped on social media and saw that the aforementioned former landlord had posted a cute little house just a few miles away for rent... on Tuesday.

I saw the house that afternoon. I told my beloved the next day. I signed the lease the following day. It was that easy. No competing, no applying, not even an extra pet deposit for my two aging furry kids that had come along on my adventure with me. It was hard to imagine that this wasn't exactly what the Universe wanted to happen.

At the time we had every intention of remaining a couple. I am simply not willing to compromise my life's work for anyone or anything. Once I began to settle into my own space and once again feel only my energy, I realized that as a whole I was not happy in the relationship as it was.

As the Universe is want to do, it gave me the bread crumbs that had me see that the relationship had run its course. It was time to take another leap and leave the relationship all together--at least for now.

"What?!?!?" you might be thinking. "You've just moved half way across the country to be with this man. You gave up so much to be together. You are just going to walk away?" My short answer is "yes."

Some call it courageous. Others crazy. I call it cooperating with the Divine; the eternal life force of the universe. What is living after all but a vital force moving through this vessel we call a person.

"How I adore your defiant, rebellious heart! It knows that what for the mind is and end, is to the heart, simply another match to ignite the sacred flames. I choose death because that is the portal to new life."
  –Alana Fairchild

I had a very similar experience when I left my job and nothing – and I do mean nothing – I had planned worked out until I found the bedrock of who I am in my work of Divine Navigation®. The Universe just needed me to take the next step before it could show me why I was actually taking that step.

The universe may only give you enough vision to get you to take the first step but not necessarily anything more. Change requires the mystery, the unknown. True creation only happens in the unknown. You can't know exactly what's going to happen. If you think you know exactly what will happen you may actually be the one limiting what could happen.

Too often we only dance in the unknown when it is thrust upon us. When an outside force is dictating the adjustment, we have two basic choices – accept or resist. Most often we resist. No wonder we aren't such big fans of change!

Your other option is to initiate change yourself. This type of change can be used as a catalyst or in response to a change that has already been thrust upon you. Either way, your soul is the one driving the change. On the one hand you are unconscious; on the other conscious.

Self-initiated change is based upon fore-knowledge of the Soul. When you don't take the initiative to create the changes that will bring about the necessary adjustments and course corrections required to ensure that you become who you are meant to be change will inevitably be thrust upon you.

When changes are thrust upon us, most focus on working really hard to "get back" to where they were; to replace the apparent loss, to fill the void. Lose your job; get another. End a relationship; find another. This is absolutely what you DON'T want to do!

Whatever shape the change takes, space is being made for something more to come in. If you simply fill the space with what you are used to, you are guaranteed to go through this all over again because you thwarted what was trying to occur in the first place.

I initiated all of these changes. Some I knew I wanted. Others I knew I needed. As hard as some of them were, I knew it's what my soul needed from me. I thought I knew what would happen on the other side of the changes, but the truth is we can only ever know the very next step.

To ruthlessly effect changes – yes, your Soul can and will be ruthless as required! – the Universe will use whatever "bait" is required to get you to take the very next step. Until you do it can't line up the next step and the next one and the next one for you. To expect otherwise would be like driving down a windy road and believing you should be able to see around the next bend before you actually get there. It's just not possible until you are speeding down the road.

Being thrust, or leaping, into the unknown is always in service to the divine plan. To bring about those conditions and situations to which the personality under the urgency and agency! of the Soul must adjust itself, change is required. But if we can't know what's to happen next, what is the antidote?

Initiate often and cooperate always!

Once you know you need to make a change – do it! Don't delay. I am not suggesting you act on every fleeting thought, but once you are certain you must not deny your truth. That will only cause suffering.

Cooperate with whatever is trying to shift on its own. Bless and release whatever is trying to go. Don't try to hold on, cling or cajole. Embrace and allow whatever is wanting to enter. Release your resistance. Allow yourself to be guided to where you are mean to be.

What I've learned is that nothing changes if nothing changes. When none of the pieces on your chessboard ever move, there is not much required of you. It is only when your world is turned upside down and your sense of orientation is nowhere to be found that your mind will truly get creative. You are lulled into complacency. You are actively avoiding your Divine Destiny. It is in the uncertainty that we create new possibility. It is in adversity that we create resilience. It is in stepping forward in blind faith that we learn to trust ourselves and the universe to provide. Of course, knowing when your soul is trying to direct you certainly makes the journey a whole lot easier!

Where the current will take me or what land yet unseen that I am headed to I do not know. How all of this will turn out is still to be revealed. For now I'll enjoy the breeze caressing my face, the sun warming my skin and the weightlessness of the void between the known and the unknown.

All your wavering is due to your longing to be stable!
Look for instability until you become stable.
   –RUMI

Maybe I am a risk taker after all. I don't know if it's that I am willing to take the risk as much as I'm *not* willing to not take the risk! I'd rather risk it all to live the life that was meant for me than risk never having truly lived at all.

Rebecca Haywood

At the young age of twenty, Rebecca Haywood entered into a decennial apprenticeship with a family of shamans – renowned Toltec Curandera, Madre Sarita, and her son, best-selling author don Miguel Ruiz. Rebecca was welcomed into their home and was soon asked to carry on Madre Sarita's lineage of healing. Under their loving tutelage, she mastered the ancient rituals of Sarita's lineage and the Toltec wisdom of don Miguel's mystery school of 'Dreaming'. Rebecca has been serving individuals and groups for twenty years, offering Spiritual Coaching, Healing, Workshops and Retreats. She offers a non-denominational but powerful message that promotes a marriage of the human with Spirit; for it is Rebecca's wish that each may experience profound transformation grounded in awareness, authenticity and self-love.

Enjoy more of Rebecca's writing and find upcoming events on her website: rebeccahaywood.com.

Chapter Thirteen

THE BRIDGE

By Rebecca Haywood

Following one's heart isn't all peace, love and sushi. It doesn't always tell you what you already suspected, or lead you towards that elated feeling of flinging open new doors. Sometimes it whispers of undesirables – challenging roads and daunting changes which seem to be leading you further from your heart's desire. Sometimes we must abandon a dream in order to find it.

This is how it played out for me. As a spiritual woman in my early twenties, I was already living life according to the call of my heart. I had dropped out of college to pursue a spiritual path. I turned down a coveted job in Greece to instead travel cross-country with my aunt. I landed at the doorstep of a re-nowned Toltec Curandera, Madre Sarita, and became her most devoted disciple.

It was effortless for me. I was young, idealistic and utterly ro-mantic. I had few attachments in the worldly dream and 'time was on my side'. Money, relationship, career – the pillars of an 'adult' life--weren't yet important to me, and I trusted them to arise organically from the spiritual foundation that I had set out to cultivate. Moreover, my heart was guiding me towards what I clearly wanted. Although I was taking 'the path less traveled' and faced some fears around that, it was relatively easy for me to let my heart lead the way.

'Dancing in the unknown' was my way of life and though one might commend me for my courage, the truth is that I felt safe in its freedom. The carved roads of the known world were where I dared not venture. I was comfortable in my watery world and felt limited by the definitions of knowledge or the structures of society. Fearing form as a trap and destination as the end of the road, I held my gypsy heart up with pride. As my grandfather used to say, I drove, "in the middle of the road with my middle-finger up"!

Living with Madre Sarita answered that call to the unknown and stilled my gypsy heart. Angels, ghosts and aliens were as real to Sarita as her own skin. She called in the rains with her prayers, exorcised spirits with her rituals and eradicated illness with her psychic surgeries. Even doctors bowed to her powers of psychic diagnostics and validated the miraculous effect of her healing work.

My days with Sarita were filled with mystery, performing ancient healing rituals and channeling messages from Spirit Guides. Nighttime was even more extraordinary, as we left our bodies to 'astral travel' to other times and places. Even our communication relied on a relationship with the unknown. Sarita only spoke Spanish, and I, a pathetic attempt at Spanglish, but we formed a deep psychic connection that transcended language to such an extent that I became her official translator after a mere two weeks.

I was at home in Sarita's world and my roots were quickly taking hold. In fact, Madre Sarita became the greatest commitment of my life. When she asked me to carry on her lineage, claiming me as her spiritual granddaughter, it fired my heart into a passionate conviction. Though I had to push through the self-doubt that questioned my worthiness, it became a mission

I embraced with every cell of my being.

It was my newfound destiny, and I allowed it to consume me. There was a sense of obligation and an urgency nipping at my heels. Madre Sarita continually reminded me that she didn't have much time left before the 'Angel of Death' would come for her. "You must learn it all, Mija, and learn it well." She was a staunch teacher. Despite her relationship with the unknown, Sarita was loyal to her methods and insisted that I replicate them to a T.

I was in a shamanic medical school, taking notes, drawing diagrams and recording every teaching. I learned the anatomy of the body and of the spirit. I memorized prayers and incantations, each for specific purposes. I rose every morning at 3 a.m. to meditate and pray, and then joined her each day for a full schedule of clients, classes and temple meetings. It was a lot, but my devotion was unwavering and my determination to authentically carry on her lineage only grew with each passing day.

That's why it came as a great surprise when my heart delivered the message that it no longer wanted to work with Madre Sarita. I was meditating in a weekend workshop with Sarita's son, don Miguel Ruiz. He had prompted us to connect with the 'dream of our heart's desire', guiding us to go into our heart and listen for its message. I assumed my position of meditation and raised my vibration, directing my attention into my heart and the pulse of life emanating from its center. Though I had no specific expectation of what it would divulge to me, I was awaiting some love-filled words to bubble up into my mind and radiate, well, peace, love and sushi.

What I found was quite the contrary. The words pierced my blissful silence.

"I don't want to work with Madre Sarita anymore. You must move out of her home and start seeing your own clients."

Immediately I felt the tension of resistance and began to argue with my heart.

"But what about carrying on her lineage? What about my mission, my destiny? I still have so much to learn from her! What if she dies? What if she disowns me? For sure she can find another willing and more loyal protégé!"

Fear was rapidly moving through me, constricting my throat with the grief of losing Madre Sarita and all that she offered. As if to allow my tantrum to complete its rant, my heart remained silent and my mind moved on to all the other reasons of why it simply wasn't possible.

"Where will I live? How will I pay for rent? I don't even have a car!" It all felt so implausible. How could this possibly be my heart's desire? It made no sense.

"When have I ever led you astray?" my heart cooed. "Trust me, this is the way. In truth, you haven't been completely happy. You have been constricting yourself into her way, when you have your own way, your own evolution to bring to this lineage. You have been yearning to express this and now is the time, but you must part with her in order to find it."

Though these words resonated with some hidden place inside of me, I still felt as if I were closing a door rather than opening one. Despite my gypsy heart, I had grown attached, invested and defined by the promise that Sarita offered. My ego was now identified by this role and I was afraid of losing it. I was afraid of losing myself. Thus, for the first time in my life, I doubted the voice of my heart.

Yet, I knew my heart was right. I hadn't been happy in my studies. I had begun to feel oppressed by the defined structure of Sarita's methods. Other words wanted to pour from me in lieu of the memorized prayers. New ways of performing her rituals were attempting to sneak through me. I had grown tired of watching client after client bestow their faith unto Madre Sarita in desperation and fanaticism. I had even begun to secretly counsel her clients with tools of self-empowerment and awareness. It was dangerous territory in my mind as I never sought to disrespect Sarita in any way. I hid from her and feigned acquiescence.

However, in truth, I was doing what Sarita had invited me to do – to combine her methods with those of her son, don Miguel. She had actually told me to study with him, saying that the best healer would be one that could bring the two together. Despite her apparent devotion to her old ways, she honored the truth as I did; that clients often create or perpetuate their imbalance, and it is their own faith which initiates and sustains healing.

But I didn't have the eyes to fully see her yet and it would take years before I developed them. It was the closing of this door and the separation from Sarita that would eventually bring me closer to her than ever. For now, though, I timidly followed this bold instruction of my heart.

"Okay," I silently whispered to my heart, "I trust you."

The beautiful thing about following our heart is that, when we surrender to it, it gives us all the information we need – the map of how to get 'there' from 'here'. Though it may not satiate all of our 'need-to-knows', it gets us started in the right direction.

Upon the acceptance of my heart's invitation, images of my new life began to swirl through my mind. I saw myself in an apartment by the beach with a roommate, a car and a job as a massage therapist. It was a lovely life, and though my hand was still hesitant upon its doorknob, I began to feel that familiar excitement of the gypsy on the move.

Map in hand, it was time for action. I fully expected the ease and grace that I had come to associate with living by the heart; that things would just fall into place as if they were awaiting my arrival. But even the river of life has its eddies, rapids and slow-moving waters, its own pace of perfection. Although I eventually landed in the life that my heart presented, the path was a meandering one with a few snags along the way. Losing faith was a temptation, but I could hear my heart cheering me on, "Keep going. This is just a stepping-stone."

Massage school was one of those seemingly slow-water moments. Massage wasn't my true passion, but it soon became clear the 'why' of it all. Massage school offered me the perfect mirror for building faith in myself as healer. I was no longer an assistant; I was the practitioner with no Sarita to rely upon or to ascribe the success.

I was shy at first in receiving acclaim from my teachers and classmates, fearing the growth of ego which would surely overshadow the humility required of a healer. The turning point occurred in one of my favorite classes, Mayan Uterine Massage. We were practicing locating the position of our partner's uterus through a hands-off energy approach. The river of life had gifted me with a partner whose uterus was prolapsed due to years of being an avid jogger. The teacher confirmed my insight and then invited me to attempt to move it back into place, hovering in concern for my partner's very real imbalance.

I knew this was possible. I had seen Sarita realign spines, expel
tumors and mend broken bones. But could I do it? I pushed
the question mark out of my mind and honed my energy into
my partner's body. Slowly, I began to pull her uterus back into
place and I actually felt it move! My partner burst into tears
as she released years of trauma and I held her as the emotions
bled out. The teacher then checked the uterus position again,
looking up at me with curious eyes. "So who are you again?"
she inquired. She then offered me an apprenticeship, but I knew
that I already had the teacher I needed – clients.

Something essential happened that day. I allowed the crown of
recognition and it filled me with a newfound power. It wasn't
ego; it was faith, something Sarita had always encouraged in
me, but that had eluded me in her presence. This moment
called it out of me. It wasn't in the assurance of a teacher, but in
the need of my partner. It was no longer about me, but born of
the invitation, the yearning, the cry for healing. Like a flower
to the sun, I opened up to my power and it flowed effortlessly
through my entire being. I now knew the significance of grant-
ing myself true authority as a healer, and I spent my remaining
months of school, gathering evidence and collecting faith.

This was the opening into the essence of my heart's message-
-that I was to bring an evolution to this lineage of healing. I
wasn't just collecting faith; I was implementing it. Under the
guise of massage therapy, I was conducting energy work without
the pretext of shamanism. It became a playground in which I
could practice freely and simply. It required no elaborate prayers
or rituals, no psychic readings or surgery. In this way, I discovered the power of pure intent unattached to form and this
became the spark that would inspire the evolution my heart had
divined.

Fanning that spark, life swiftly delivered a thriving private practice. Now that I was on my own turf, I was able to expand beyond my secret energy work and invite Sarita's methods to the playground. I was inspired and emboldened. The loyalty that once held me to Sarita's way had waned into a beautiful honoring of what I came to call "formless healing". I allowed each healing to flow from that place of pure intent – the faith drawn out of me by the call of the client's need.

The magic that ensued was beyond my imagination. Prayers emerged from my lips that spoke, not in my language of faith, but in that of my clients, and with divined messages that touched the hidden stories within them. The healing rituals came alive for me and I within them, roused by some unseen hand that reached through me and directly into the client. Each healing was like a dance, bending with the movement of the moment and to the song of the client's body, mind and spirit.

It seemed that I had met the demands of my heart. Even Madre Sarita honored my mastery by inviting me to lead workshops with her. This was the final piece and the bridge that would bring me home. As I stepped into the role of teacher, I found the eyes to discern the significance of Sarita's methods and of form all together.

I saw how students needed to at least start with a defined form and how it had served my own evolution as a healer. Until one fully develops faith in themselves and in the realm of infinite possibility, the form offers a crutch to lean on. The prayers and rituals help to distract the reasoning mind from its doubts and engage it into the healing; like giving the squirrel of the mind a nut to chew so that the larger mind can get to work. By giving students a distinct structure with the promise of results, it eased their faith into action. Even if that faith was being placed outside of oneself, it was a start and an opening to the greater truth.

Ultimately, form served both healer and client by providing a solidity in which each could place their faith – a language they could hear, a ritual they could feel. Perception was the portal that ushered the un-manifest into the manifest matter of the client's body. Beyond power of faith, it was the experience that made it real and offered a physical memory to displace the ghosts of their imbalance.

In truth, Sarita's way and mine required form in order to deliver their intent. The only difference was that my "formless healing" bent to the faith of the client, whereas Sarita's way was a pre-determined structure that called upon their faith. Either way, prayer and ritual – language and action – were the vessels of the seed pod, delivering new life unto earth. It was the alchemy of faith and form that allowed the healing to bear fruit.

This was the bridge my heart was waiting for me to cross – the place where faith and form come together. The young woman who had sought the unknown by rebelling against form had surrendered. Her watery world had found a riverbed in which she could flow freely, cradled by earth and lifted by sky into rain. I was finally able to stand in both worlds of the known and the unknown, embracing each as necessary and beautiful expressions of this human experience. I had become the bridge between the two.

I was now at peace with the knowing that I could honor this lineage of healing in an authentic way. The evolution I obtained was truly a return to its origin. Sarita had known all along and gracefully allowed my journey of discovery. Though she no longer walks this earth in body, her lineage continues on through me and through all those she touched.

I had come full circle. Through the apparent departure from a dream, I had arrived to the heart of it. It required awareness, courage and conviction, but most of all, it called upon a trust in my heart and a willingness to navigate by the mystery of the unknown.

Joel Crandall

Joel Crandall, Kinesiologist and Exercise Physiologist, graduated from SUNY-Cortland in 1991. He has dedicated his life fine tuning and mastering innovative advancements in Exercise Science, Biomechanical Harmony and Structural Joint Balancing at PhysioCareCenter- Injury, Pain, Prevention and Performance Clinic in Los Angeles, California. He is also the creator of the VOILÀ Method of Structural Joint Balancing.

VOILA Method of Structural Joint Balancing is new innovative way of helping the body heal itself! VOILA Method balances the Keystones, in harmony. during static and dynamic movement to create equilibrium and dynamic kinesthetic stability for increased performance and a pain-free life.

Joel is available sharing the knowledge and education through hands on classes, clinics, workshops and seminars on the The VOILÀ Method of Structural Joint Balancing.

Chapter Fourteen

MY LIFE AS A CONCUSSED HUMAN: MY JOURNEY TO RECOVERY

By Joel Crandall

At three years old I had my first memory. I was wearing red pants and green hoodie sweatshirt and walking around a rose bush to go into the house. I heard a voice in my head say, "What are you doing here?" This story, as I found out, is WHY I am here.

Many people will tell themselves, "I'm just tired", "I can't seem to remember anything today" or "I'm not thinking straight today".

Most of us don't realize how much of a Brain Fog we are in until its lifted.

Now that my fog has been lifted. I can see and think more clearly and creatively.

This is how it all began. When I was about eight years old, a few friends and I decided it would be fun to take my wagon down a trail on the side of a hill that went down to the creek bed where we used to play.

Well, we made it a few yards when we lost control and rolled down the hill. My friend was lucky enough to be stopped by a tree. I, on the other hand, made it all the way to the bottom, hit a hard embankment and landed flat on my back on a large flat slab of rock. I was knocked out cold. That was my first severe concussion.

In high school, I had my "bell" rung and saw "stars" a few times, but at that time not much was known about concussions. I never considered them to be more than bad headaches.

In my sophomore year of college, we were having our traditional Red/White scrimmage at the end of football training camp, before the season opener. Got the call to run the ball up the middle. There was a huge gaping hole, but one of the lineman was able to get his hand on my foot to trip me up. As I fell forward, I put my hand down on the ground to regain my balance and lifted up my head to drop my hips to regain control. Just then, the safety, with a perfectly legal hit at the time, went helmet-to-helmet with me with such force it brought my legs through and under me to where I ended up in a seated position on the ground. Everything went white. Bright white.

The strangest feeling occurred at that moment. I felt as if I were outside of my body, hovering above and looking down upon myself. I watched as I handed the ball to Head Coach Dennis Kaiser, and then I watched myself walk off the field. I believe I knew this was going to be the last time I ever played football.

The football team had after a few days off before the season began. I returned to practice thinking everything was fine, even though, in truth, I didn't feel well. Vaguely I remember struggling through warm ups. We broke into offense and defense drills. I ran a simple toss sweep to the left, and as I went to cut up field I fell down with no one around me. The coach yelled out to run it again. I took the pitch and ran around the left edge and again I fell down. Something wasn't allowing me to keep my balance and make the cut.

I walked over to the athletic trainer. I said, "Something is wrong, I can't feel my feet touching the ground." As I was talking to him, he noticed my head kept bobbing. I was unaware I was doing this, but I saw the look of concern on his face as asked me what was going on. I remember replying that the helmet felt too heavy. He sent me into the athletic training room, which was about 100 yards away from the practice field. I made it about halfway there when I got a back/neck spasm that dropped me to my knees. I ended up crawling on my hands and knees the rest of the way into the training room. It must have taken me twenty minutes.

When I got there, the trainers threw ice packs from my neck all the way down my back. They gave me this treatment for a few weeks, but I wasn't getting much better. I was still having difficulty holding my head up with the weight of the helmet. Reluctantly I decided to end my days of playing football. Ironically, that team, after many losing season, went undefeated that year in 1988 – the first time in the Cortland State Red Dragons history.

Depression set in, as my lifelong dream of making a career of playing football ended. I went to see the Team Sport Psychologist, Dr. William F. Straub. I will forever be grateful for Dr. Straub taking me under his wing and helping me. He spent time with me and developed a meditation tape for me. To this day, I still use this meditation which included the mantra: "I am consistently confident in myself, at all times and in all situations."

Dr. Straub asked me listen to it every day for three weeks, which I did diligently. I was then to come help him film the next home football game.

I will never forget walking into the Chugger Davis stadium to meet up with Dr. Straub. The first thing he said to me was, "You have been listening to the tape! I saw you walking from 100 yards away." He could see I was carrying myself differently – chest up, proud, confident and walking with purpose.
I spent quite a bit of time with Dr. Straub that year and still call him once a year to thank him.

The rest of college was a fog. I had difficulty sitting and studying, needing to walk around the dorm room as my roommate dictated notes to me. When I took tests, I would have to remember where I was when I heard that information or what the page my class notes looked like to get the correct answers.

Cortland State is a great teaching university. My major was Physical Education (now called Kinesiology) and my goal was to be a teacher. It was a very science intensive program. As a matter of fact our professors of Anatomy, Dr. Spence and Dr. Mason, wrote our textbook. They also taught at nearby Cornell University, and graded us Cortland students harder than they did the Ivy leaguers that were going to be heading to medical school.

There were many great professors at Cortland, but I started to excel when I met Dr. Charles Ash, a professor of exercise physiology. I decided to stay an extra year in college to minor in exercise science with him. I never had to study for the class because he was very dynamic in his teaching. I was able to recall his teachings and I was living the lifestyle of exercise science. He had this knack of providing an answer that was just

out of reach of your current knowledge base but within grasp
if you did the work of thinking and searching for it. I like to
think I do this to this day with attendees of the Voila Seminars.

After college, there was a recession. I was doing part time teaching gigs when I received a call from a summer school roommate. He asked if I wanted to move to California to do private
training in a gym that he was opening.

In college, I had always said I would never move to California because that was the fitness capital of the world. I figured
anybody there would have way more knowledge that I had ac-
quired at my small Northeastern college.

However, there was nothing holding me to my tiny hometown
of McDonough, with a population of 700 (though I swear there
was a parade in town the day they counted). We had five paved
roads and three stop signs in the entire town. My sister, Tess,
worked for the airlines at the time and got me a ticket to Los
Angeles. I packed two bags with all my belongings and a small
pocketful of money ($200) and off to California I went. I had
nothing to lose. I think my parents thought I would return
home within a week or two.

Upon landing at LAX, my friend picked me up at airport. It
was culture shock. Los Angeles was HUGE. I asked, "How do
you know how to get around here?" He handed me a Thomas
Bros guide, a thick book with about 400 pages of maps of the
city of Los Angeles. (Remember, these were the days before
GPS.)

Luckily we were staying in the small beach city of Hermosa
Beach. This gave me a little time to transition a bit before tack-
ling my trip to Hollywood where the gym was located.

It turned out I would be working in the old Jane Fonda work-out gym, which now had a new name and new owners.

We finished the work on the gym and started personal training at the gym. Things were starting to take off. One of my clients was Salma Hayek, before she became the big international star she is today.

She was also my last client I trained at that gym.

Three weeks after moving to Los Angeles, I was a passenger in a motorcycle accident. A car turned in front of us in an intersection and we T-boned the car. I was not wearing a helmet. Flying through the air, I had that same feeling of being outside of my body as I did on the football field, watching myself twist and flip through the air.

I was required to take three gymnastic classes in college. At 6'2" and 212 pounds I was a bit too big and tall to be a gymnast and it was no surprise that I wasn't very good at it. Yet I swear those gymnastic classes saved my life. I was spotting the ground, the sky, the ground, the sky, the ground. Yes, two flips with one twist. I didn't quite stick the landing, falling like Superman on one knee and fist. As I landed I tucked and rolled over my shoulder. Momentum carried me back to my feet as I tried to run to get out of the street. I realized my right leg was not working and was forced to hop to the curb on one leg.

Then I collapsed onto the sidewalk.

It took months to recover from my broken patella. I had lost four inches off of my thigh. But it was time to try to find work. I limped into a gym and asked for an application. I was leaving to fill out the application, when a woman asked me to stay and fill it out there. I did just that and after clocking out, in the woman sat down to talk with me. "You look new here," she said. I told her who I was and what had happened to me. After our talk, she told me I could use her as a reference. That's how I met Tracy Statler, who was a sport psychologist for the 2016 USA Olympic team. Oh, and I got the job at the gym as a trainer.

In class discussion with a group of personal trainers in training for a large gym, Sport Club LA, I had an epiphany. These trainers were from large universities such as USC, UCLA, and Cal State Los Angeles. As I sat there and participated in the discussion, I noticed that they were looking at me like I had three heads. I asked them why. They replied, "We have no idea what you are talking about." I mentioned that they should have learned this basic knowledge in second semester of college. They said that they had never learned what I was talking about. (I wish I could recall the topic). At that point, I was very proud of my Cortland State education! That feeling of inferiority I had from having come from a small school suddenly evaporated.

Years later, at a gym in Beverly Hills, I was training a chiropractor who asked me if I ever thought of going to massage school. Coming from a small town, I asked, "What is that?" I had never had a massage in my life and didn't know what it was about. I was intrigued, though, and after checking it out ended up enrolling in massage school, The Institute for Psycho-Structural Balancing.

The IPSB believed in treating the body as a whole. One class I took was about Energy work – Polarity. I wasn't sold on the concept until after I tried it and I could feel the energy in my hands and around me. When it was my turn to receive the work, I had my eyes closed and the person was bringing their hands towards my head. I cried, out, "Stop right there. You're hurting me!"

The man said with surprise, "I'm twelve inches away from your head."

I replied, "I know, because I am keeping you that far away."

Without realizing it, I was on to something. But even then I didn't dive into that realm of bodywork until the VOILA Method was downloaded to me as the messenger.

With all my studies and searching for ways to help my clients, I was still dealing with the effects of all my concussions and I was getting worse. I was helping other people but I had no way of helping myself.

That is, until my mom passed away and the VOILA Method was downloaded and I found the way to help myself. It turned out I was dealing with the debilitating post-concussion conditions, PTVS (Post Traumatic Vision Syndrome) and PTSD (Post Traumatic Stress Disorder). I was losing my memory. I was depressed. I had major brain fog. Reading was difficult. I was now in my late 30's, and even though I was very athletic and had an athletic build, working out caused me pain. For me, working out was a double-edged sword. It would take me a week to recover because my body had to work harder to compensate for my lack of equilibrium caused by the concussions. Injuries were occurring more and more often.

The VOILA Method changed all that.

VOILA Method of Structural Joint Balancing is new innovative way of helping the mind/body in healing itself by restoring the mind/body to its natural state of Harmony! VOILA Method is a complete Mind/Body System. VOILÀ Assessment is systematic, yet it is a dynamic and fluid Mind/Body assessment that is done throughout the entire session and is treatment tool to assist the practitioner in saving time and getting long lasting results by finding the true cause of loss of equilibrium in the Mind/Body.

When developing the VOILA Method, my major incentive was my own recovery, but I would come to see the extent of how it could help others get back their lives. It certainly changed mine. I have been excited by the development of VOILA Method.

It is so much fun watching the faces of clients change, but for me the excitement is watching the development of the VOILA Method practitioners, how they are able to not only use the practice successfully in their clinics, but also in their and their family's lives.

It took quite a few years, and I didn't realize it at the time, but that was my awakening. I didn't lose myself on that practice field, I found my SELF. I now have the answer to the question I first asked myself when I was three years old. Why am I here? To help and teach myself and others how to heal from the inside.

Melette Evans

Melette Evans is a fearless adventurer who wants to spend her life surrounded by creative, loving, passionate souls with whom she can work and play. Her motto: "Helping create happier lives one person at a time"

A humanist with a mind equally designed for science and the aesthetic, Melette has worked for over thirty years to enhance the lives of everyone she meets in many different ways. From caring for hospital Emergency Room and Surgical patients and their families in a compassionate manner, to creating exquisite home / work spaces that enhance the everyday living experience for her design company's clients; and protecting the privacy and security of companies and individuals with her technical computer skills, Melette's mission is to leave each individual she encounters with a positive experience, however small it may be.

A writer and visionary, she's the founder of Bevylife.com, a beautifully crafted website bringing together singles who desire the ability to make deeper and more meaningful connections within their communities. This resource that connects like-minded singles supports Melette's deep belief that everyone leads a happier life when they feel as though they matter and have a place to belong.

When she's not writing or working, Melette can be found in some far-flung country discovering new friendships, enjoying unique experiences and making new memories.

Look for Bevylife to be featured on the new hit show, *Radical Dating*, slated for release Fall 2017.

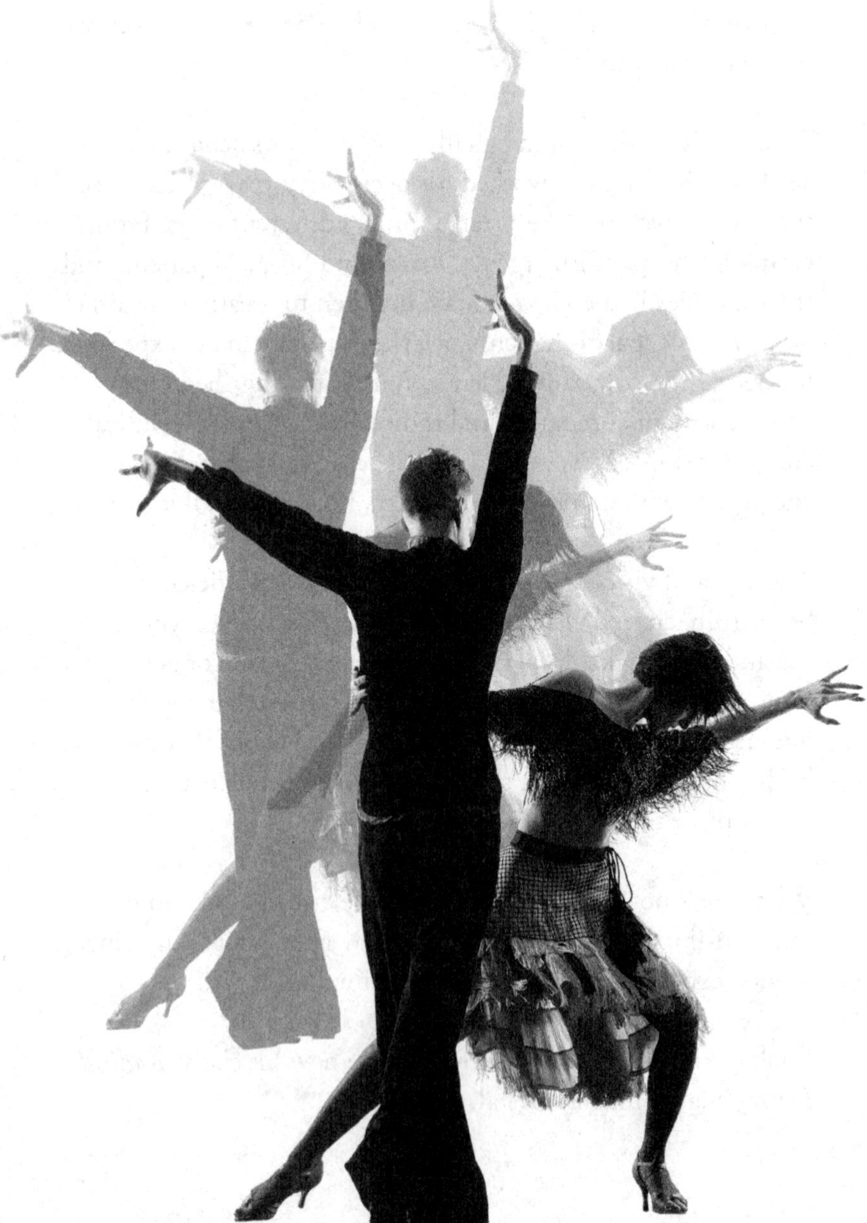

Chapter Fifteen

DANCING IN THE RABBIT HOLE

By Melette Evans

Like most young ones, when I was a little kid I was afraid of the dark. But unlike my childhood friends, rather than sending me running in the opposite direction and into the safety of the sunlight, shadowy unknown places invited me in. I couldn't resist going behind forbidden closed doors and into spooky rooms where anything imaginable could be hiding. As fearful as I was, the unknown held a sort of magical allure for me that none of my faithful comrades seemed to appreciate. I felt like Alice in Wonderland, and believed that falling into those mysterious deep, dark rabbit-holes would eventually lead me to fascinating people, places and things if I could just get to the other side. It wasn't until decades later, and after many harrowing trips down rabbit holes that my fear of the dark finally started to fade away. That's when learned I could get through almost anything, and come out better for having had the experience.

Mom and Dad always told me I was smart and that I could be whatever I wanted to be. Like the other young girls in my circle, I did all the "right" things. I went to university, studied hard and landed a good job. I met a "nice" man, had a beautiful wedding and together, we began building a new home. Over the course of our short marriage though, I began to learn that my husband Brett was not the man I thought he was.

The house, its sense of permanence and security and my belief that it would promise future happiness provided a distraction from what was missing in my marriage, and from my husband's dark side. I hoped that once we moved into our new home, the drinking sprees, fits of rage and emotional void that had steadily worsened since we married would all disappear. One day, while driving to view the construction progress, I heard the news that the space shuttle Challenger had exploded and there were no survivors. As my heart ached for the astronauts who had lost their lives, I realized that no matter what you do or how you plan, life can be irrevocably changed or even destroyed, in an instant.

Our third wedding anniversary was two months after the Challenger tragedy. I had purchased a romantic card and present for Brett, and was hoping for a kind gesture in return to show that he loved me. Looking forward to a special evening, I ran up the three flights of stairs to our apartment, gift in hand, only to find our front door wide open and my husband standing in our almost-empty living room. I thought we had been robbed until my husband declared, "I'm leaving you. My attorney will be calling." Then he was gone. My entire world – everything I knew and had planned for – had disappeared in a matter of seconds.

I have little memory of the next three days other than a hazy sense of pain so intense, I couldn't eat or drink. On day four, I summoned the strength to shower and drive to my office. When I stopped to buy gas, both of our joint credit cards were rejected. I was sure there was a mistake since we always paid our bills on time. I found enough change in my purse to pay for a gallon of gas, enough to get me to work and to the bank to fix the problem with our credit cards and then home. But when I got to the bank, the teller told me there was only one dollar left in each of our accounts. The next day I confirmed that Brett had not only cleaned out our home of all personal items, he had emptied our cash, retirement and investment accounts and closed our credit cards, leaving me too broke to buy food or gas, much less anything else. I had to borrow $1,000 from my parents for bare necessities, and as I moved back into my childhood bedroom, I descended into a deep, even suicidal, depression.

I was sinking into in a downward spiral and could see no way out. Yet, through the darkness, often I heard a faint, comforting voice say, "Everything will be alright… just get to the other side." I thought I must be losing my mind, but after a while I began to listen, to trust this guidance. I realized that the reassuring voice was coming from within me.

After a month, that calming inner voice helped me get my act together enough to attend my boss' wedding. As one of the groomsman escorted me to my seat, sparks flew between us and magic filled the air. Our relationship quickly escalated, and within weeks, we were making promises for the future. The flowers, affectionate words and romantic gestures he lavished upon me "proved" we were in love and compelled me to ignore subtle signs of anger and verbal abuse. Soon, I was married again, and constructing a house that was even bigger and better than the last one. I would actually get to move into this one. But not for long.

One crisp October day, several months after we had moved into our new home, I stopped to survey the budding lawn we had planted, the bright emerald blades of grass emerging from the rich soil. The beauty of it brought a smile to my face and I convinced myself it signaled a fresh start to my life and my marriage. Happy thoughts flooded my mind as I drove to work. Little did I know that mere minutes later, my life would

implode even more catastrophically than before.

At work, I was abruptly handed my final paycheck and thank-lessly escorted to the door, the result of a company layoff. My stomach churned and my head pounded on the drive back home, in fearful anticipation of my husband's reaction to learning that I was no longer bringing home a paycheck, of how he would blame me and what he would do to me. I was so distracted I did not see the Ford F-700 make an illegal turn directly in front of me. In a deafening blur of screeching tires and crunching metal, my red Honda Prelude smashed into the truck, nearly head-on.

My emotional injuries were worse than my physical ones and I refused to be taken to the hospital. I watched as my crumpled car was lifted onto the tow truck, then allowed the police officer to drive me home. I had planned to call my husband once I got there but it turned out I didn't have to. Walking in bruised and broken, I found him there, cheating on me with another wom-an. Worse yet, soon afterwards he became the father of her child.

This time, I found the courage to be the one to walk away, and I did – far away from my husband and into a new, successful, $250,000+ a year job. I also got a wonderful companion, my beloved Siberian Husky, Sasha. Soon, my successes at work took me overseas, and while I hated having to leave Sasha with my parents, I was thrilled at exploring fascinating, exotic places. But even as I tried to find a way back to myself, instead, I land-ed once again with another abusive man.

It was in London that I met Michael. Tall, dark and of Greek descent, he had the handsome chiseled features and well-de-veloped musculature of a statue of Adonis. He took my breath away. Soon, I was living another fairy tale; a current-day Cinderella protectively courted, showered with compliments, even invited to the annual Lord Mayor's ball – an invitation of greater social prominence than I could ever have imagined receiving. Michael proudly showed me off to English high society, and within two months he told me he loved me and urged me to move in with him and start planning our wedding. Being the ever-faithful girlfriend, I did.

Once we settled into his flat, however, his protective behavior turned jealous, possessive and controlling. He told me where to go and what to do, even on which side of the refrigerator to put "my food." After several of my dresses mysteriously went missing, Michael informed me he had discarded all of my apparel that he considered unsuitable. As swiftly as our relationship had developed, it began to unravel, leaving me with a sick but familiar feeling at the pit of my stomach.

Then Michael's friend, Paul, asked to speak to me to help plan a surprise birthday celebration for Michael. But the birthday party was never mentioned. Paul wanted to warn me about Michael, to tell me to be careful because his friend's treatment of women was not what it should be. He explained that none of Michael's previous relationships had lasted more than a few weeks before Michael decided his girlfriend of the moment was too flawed to keep around. He dropped each one in pursuit of his next conquest, leaving them emotionally – and sometimes physically – damaged. I thanked Paul for his concern and for risking his friendship to tell me the truth, and I promised I would keep our meeting a secret.

I was determined that this time I would learn from my previous experiences, and rather than wait for months in agony, I would face the darkness head-on. My plan was to carry on as normal

until I returned from a business trip to Brussels at the end of
the week. Then I would move out while Michael was at work
and avoid his rage and retaliation at my leaving him.

I returned to London on a rainy Thursday afternoon and was
completely soaked by the time I walked the short distance home
from the train station. Michael should have been there, but
the flat was dark and quiet. I lugged the heavy suitcase up the
stairs to our bedroom and switched on the light. Something was
different but I couldn't immediately sense what was wrong. As
I started to unpack, I found my dresser drawers and wardrobe
were all empty. Looking to the desk, I noticed my computer
and everything else I had left there was gone too. My personal
items had been emptied from the medicine cabinet; even my
shampoo from the shower was gone. Any shred of evidence that
I had lived in that flat had been removed, including food I had
left in the refrigerator. It was as if I had been erased. In a panic,
I ran from room to room and finally, in a small spare storage
area, I found some of my clothes and personal items piled on
the floor beside an air mattress with a note from Michael stating
that I was being assigned "this room" and for the privilege of
staying there I needed to pay him £ 3,000 in back rent. Searching further, I found the few pieces of antique furniture that I
had brought to the flat with me shoved into the small garage.
But I was unable to find my computer, my jewelry or my few
other valuables.

I knew I needed to do something extreme to recover my items
and save myself from this situation. Michael's connections
extended far beyond the social scene, to the London police
and other governmental agencies. Not fully knowing what I
was looking for, I began searching his desk drawer, my heart
pounding, terrified that at any moment he could come through
the door and catch me. In a zippered case of official looking

documents, I found the contact card of his superior agent of his covert government job. Summoning all the confidence I could muster, I dialed the number. I had no idea what I would say, hoping there would be an answer and at the same time hoping there wouldn't. A gruff voice on the other end barked, "Chief Agent Ward." I took a deep breath and calmly explained that I was Michael's former girlfriend and that I did not want to cause him any trouble, but that Michael had taken my valuable belongings and I wanted them back. I told Ward I knew that he, as Michael's superior agent, could facilitate my request and I would greatly appreciate his assistance in the matter. Further, if my valuables were not brought back to me within two hours, I would call every news station and hold a public press conference about the dishonest activities committed against me by a member of this agency and the complicity of that agent's superiors. If my belongings were promptly returned, I would drop the matter and keep it all confidential. Ward condescendingly replied, "That is a very serious accusation that you are making young lady, against one of our government agents." I replied in an equally condescending tone, "And it is a very serious act that your agent committed." After a long pause, Ward said, "Give me thirty minutes," and hung up.

I could barely breathe. What had I done? I didn't even know the actual agency I had called or what bombshell was going to be dropped on me. I paced the floor for what seemed like forever, but thirty minutes later, I heard the squealing tires of multiple vehicles approaching. I rushed outside to find five black Mercedes parked in a half circle around our front door. Michael emerged from the car closest to the house. He went to the trunk, then came toward me with two boxes under one arm and a gun in the other hand. Stopping just inches in front of me, he dropped the boxes at my feet. Inside them were my computer, jewelry and other valuables. As he got back in the car he shot me a look of complete disdain and said, "I'll deal with you later."

One by one the cars peeled off. As soon as I was sure they were gone, I called a moving company and arranged to pay six times the normal fee to have them collect my belongings and ship them to the United States that night. I quit my job, booked the next available flight home and never saw Michael again.

I emerged from that rabbit hole a little less damaged than I had from my previous Wonderland tours. Back in the States, and still riding high professionally, I settled into what felt like the perfect place for me – Boulder, Colorado. I bought a cute little house near the mountains. I loved where I lived. I had my job, and I was reunited with my beloved Sasha; she was my constant companion, my precious baby. All I needed now, I thought, was the perfect man with whom I could gaze upon the sunsets and live a normal, happy life.

I hoped I had finally learned to avoid the dark places, or at least to recognize their depths before diving in. This time, however, the darkness came for me. In a big way.

When the 2008 financial crisis hit, I lost my job, my house and the savings it had taken me years to rebuild. Sasha and I moved into a dank basement apartment and ate food from a local food bank. I made what little money I could cleaning houses. But with the affection and companionship of my Sasha, and the lessons learned from previous hardships, I persisted and survived instead of crumbling under the stress.

Then I lost Sasha too. Her kidneys failing… I couldn't let her suffer. Gently rocking her in my arms and stroking her soft paws as the vet helped her slip away, I looked into her sweet, crystal blue eyes and said a final goodbye to my best and most loyal friend.

I might have slipped away then, too, if not for the lifeline cast from a dear friend offering me a job in San Diego. For five long years, I worked at that job, but I wasn't thriving. The love and support of my friend kept me going, but my heart remained in Colorado. That was my home. Although my desire for a romantic relationship was as strong as ever, I made no effort to meet anyone in San Diego because I knew I didn't belong there.

This time though, I didn't wait for life to happen to me. Instead, I began to write my own fairy tale, my own Wonderland fantasy in which I lived in Colorado – even if only part time at first-- with a new furry companion, wonderful friends, meaningful and enjoyable work and a beautiful home. As I focused on what I wanted instead of my current reality, my life began to evolve.

First, my sweet Ragdoll kitten, Sophie, came bouncing into my life, bringing much needed joy and laughter. Then an opportunity arose with my company to work remotely, from anywhere. Guess where I chose? Colorado. The constant travel between Denver and San Diego was not easy, but I cherished every moment in my treasured state. I met friends and rented a wonderful house with a back yard big enough for a sister for Sophie, a new Husky puppy. At times, I felt as though I was moving one step forward and two steps back, but I kept going, knowing I could rise above each challenge, and that great things would await me once I got to the other side. I kept living and writing my story and believing and focusing on all the wonderful things that would come into my experience.

It wasn't until I built my own company, based on connecting people and forging community to enhance people's lives, that I truly appreciated the gifts the darkness and uncertainty in my life had given me. We all face dark times that feel impossible to bear, but the strength we gain from those desperate times is what allows us to get to the other side, to write our own happy endings, and finally, to emerge from the rabbit hole into the light.

Wayne D. Carter

From his first career spanning a decade as an award-winning sound engineer and tour manager in the music industry, through starting and growing a successful construction company, to his training in neuro-psychology, Wayne D. Carter has always followed the road less traveled, sometimes even by choice. Over the years, Wayne has worked to unite his body, mind and spirit through intensive study and training. The result is a man who sees far, with eyes and soul, who senses what is unsaid, and who is open to experiencing the world in ways outside the norm. He is currently writing a book and having far-ranging adventures with his dog, Soulo.

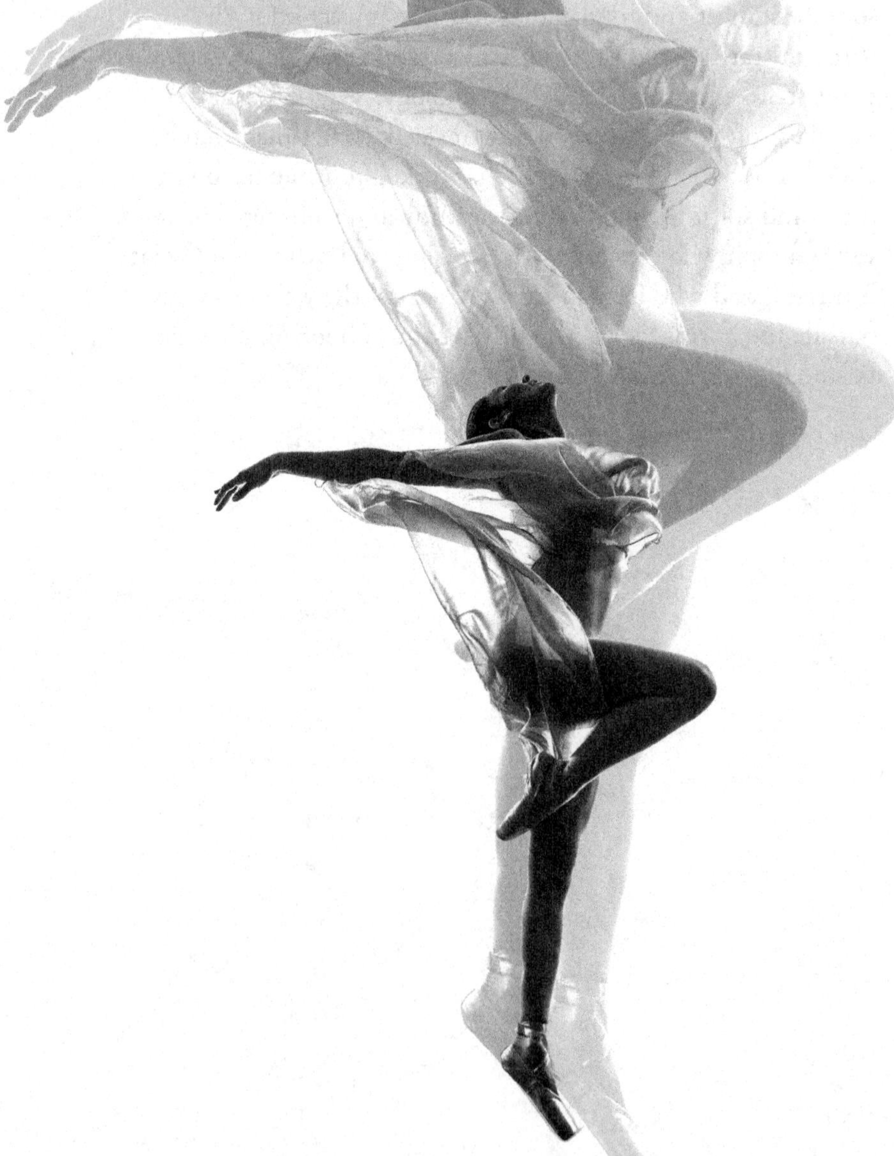

Chapter Sixteen

DISCOVERING LOVE IS EVERYWHERE AND ALL THE TIME

By Wayne D. Carter

The Mercedes came into my lane. The side panel of the car grabbed my front tire. The panicked driver punched the gas to race away, shaking me back and forth, over and over. I don't know how long this went on: it seemed like a long time, but also like no time at all. Finally, he broke free and raced off, out of my sight.

That's when things started to get weird.

I knew I had a button for emergency flashers, but had no idea how to locate it. This seemed odd to me, even then. I ran my fingers over every inch of the dashboard, searching as if I were blind. Success! I turned on the flashers. That task accomplished, I was able to take a moment and look around me. The world seemed to have a shimmer to it, as if it had been filmed through gauze, like a glamorous movie star. As I got out of the truck, I didn't feel pain or panic. I just noticed feeling surreal. I was lost in my own mind.

Fortunately, I was aware enough to go to the hospital. But it is a mark of my mental state that I decided I could drive myself there. I don't remember that drive, but I vividly remember standing in front of the doors, having no idea how a door worked or how to get in. I was not afraid. Mostly I was puzzled, and unwilling to admit that things were very wrong. I felt blissful, smiling even as I had to ask security how to open the door.

I checked in, saying I'd been in an accident. Doors continued to mystify me. They kept asking me if I had been drinking, though I repeatedly told them I had not.

Eventually, through the hospital and my doctor, I was diagnosed with Post-Concussion Syndrome, also known as Traumatic Brain Injury (TBI). These diagnoses changed everything. I could not even drive, let alone pursue the fourth year of my PhD program in Neuropsychology. My marriage fell apart, and my careers in construction and mental health both took significant hits. It was during these dark times that I turned toward love.

I started off relearning and practicing Self Love. I had always known myself to be highly intelligent and hyper competent. In the months after my injury, no one knew how much of that I would recover, least of all me. I had to learn to love this new self who sometimes struggled with things that had always come easily to me. I had to honor my new limits.

Help came from many people along my journey, and I am sure there are many more than I can remember. I learned how to receive, and even more difficult, I learned how to ask for help from others. The first person I had to ask was my wife. I was not allowed to drive, but Dee took me to parking lots to practice in order to safely re-learn this skill that had been second nature to me. I had to apologize to friends when I forgot their birthdays, or even when I didn't know whether I had attended their party and just couldn't remember, or if I'd missed it altogether. It was humbling.

As I got better, I planned a journey for myself and my beloved dog, Hunter. The journey would teach me to know and respect my limits, to take things one step at a time and to allow the generosity of others to assist me along the way.

In planning my trip, the doctors limited me to 100 miles a day, a far cry from driving 700 miles at a time the way I used to. I planned a route that would take me 3,000 miles, stopping along the way to visit friends, to park my trailer and camp and visit places from my past. It would not have been ambitious for my former self, but my new circumstances presented challenges I believed I could manage and ones that would help me grow. I was excited for the freedom this would bring, while also feeling fear of what could go wrong.

The first friends I visited lived in Twisp, Washington, in the beautiful Okanogan region. Not long before my arrival, a wildfire had swept through the area, destroying many homes. Fortunately, my friends' home was spared, but they lost outbuildings, and the whole place looked flat and lifeless. It seemed like an especially apt metaphor, as both the land and I were ready for re-birth.

I had known Vern and Joanne for a long time, but somehow, I could remember only Vern's name. My brain had no access to Joanne's. I was grateful that they were gracious about that faux pas and loved me just the way they always had. Their support helped me continue on my journey toward independence and self-discovery.

My next segment would take me up to British Columbia, where I had friends who had invited me to stay for several days. At this point, I knew it would exceed my limit of 100 miles a day, but I

decided I could manage it and set off.

I headed out, and saw a road that went north. Thinking it would save miles and time, I impulsively turned onto it. I drove for some time, but the route did not turn out as I had expected. Not wanting to backtrack, I asked for directions and was told that there was a one lane road that would take me back to the highway. Well, what I was actually told was, "Take a right by the tavern," which is a perfect example of getting directions in a small, rural town. I followed the instructions and had a beautiful drive. Although the road was narrow, and there were no guard rails between me and the water, I felt anxiety fall away from me to be replaced by love.

Everything I saw was with new eyes on that day. I came to a T in the road with no idea which way to go. What I remember most is not that I didn't know where I was. Instead, I remember the whiteness of the gravel on the road as it reflected the sun. I remember the beauty of the mountains and lakes I passed; even the devastation of a rockslide had its own beauty. I remember being open to Love.

Somehow, though, that all changed as I came back into civilization. I had hoped to find cell service and GPS when I finally reached a town, but it was unavailable to me. That meant I had to ask for help once again… from a stranger; one who would hear me stutter and watch as I searched for words that would not come to mind. I began to once again doubt my value, my very right to exist in a world where I felt I was of no use. The anxiety came rushing back, and the peace of that drive was all but lost. Even now, writing this, my body remembers the fear I felt as I walked into a gas station to ask for directions. "I'm lost," I said, and that was absolutely true.

Thanks to their directions, I was back where I needed to be fairly quickly. After a brief and pleasant border crossing, I was in Canada, and soon was safely at the home of my friends. They kindly took care of grocery shopping, and getting my phone ready for the Canadian network with a new SIM card; more expressions of love in a concrete form that was hard to ignore.

Nature often provides a gateway into love. As I set up my camp, a crow visited me, chatting to me in a way that made me feel loved. I later learned that he had been injured as a young bird, rescued and healed by humans, and never lost his affinity for communicating with my species, maybe even believing himself to be one of us. It was a great welcome to British Columbia and the lessons nature would continue to provide.

I brought a camera and kept photographic and written records of my journey. I wanted to remember it as well as possible, and to be able to go back later to remind myself of the lessons and stories I gathered along the way.

Photography was an important part of documenting my journey. I remember times when photographing nature, I would notice how beautiful it could be in its imperfection. More important to my personal experience was how well it adapted to the reality of its circumstances. The trees knocked askew by the rockslide had lost limbs, had been broken, had been shifted from their previously solid ground, and yet, they continued to heal and grow. The wisdom they showed me was necessary to my own survival; they pointed to my path forward.

I'd like to say that the lesson was offered and received all at once, but that's not how it happened. There were times when my self-pity rose above my knowledge and ability to keep it at bay. There were times when my own lack of basic competence

was the cause of my fear.

One night, after driving all day, I arrived in the town where I was to camp for the night. Hunter and I split a cheeseburger and fries at a small burger place. After we ate, we drove up and down the streets of this small town, trying to find the campground. Over and over again, I looked and could not find it. Darkness was falling. I called the camp for directions, but at that point, even knowing where I was headed didn't help. I was scared. I was scared of my brain and of the roads, I was afraid there wouldn't be a gas station. I was ashamed of being a grown man who felt unable to manage what used to be simple tasks and the feelings that now came along with them.

I returned to the burger place. It felt safe to me, as I knew where I was. I calmed down enough to call the campground again. As I haltingly explained myself, the owner said he remembered talking to me, and he offered to drive out and let me follow him back. I felt astonished by this act of kindness and acceptance, and by the lush camping space with a beautiful view. I slept well that night, once again knowing I was surrounded by love. I had always been the helper, the one to come to the aid of others. Now, I was learning to receive.

I woke up twelve hours later and began my journey again. There were stops along the way, meals eaten, supplies purchased and kindness everywhere. There were the strangers on a narrow road who took the time to warn me of a herd of horses ahead. I remember having a long conversation with a couple at a gas station; nothing extraordinary, just talk about trucks, camping, fishing and such. There was even a woman who washed, dried and folded all of my laundry, including bedding, and would accept only a token payment. In each of these encounters, I was newly aware of the connection I felt, the gift of community with other beings.

As I mentioned before, my learning was not a straight line. It zigged and zagged in all directions, sometimes soaring, sometimes plummeting. The plummet is common among people with TBI, often resulting in thoughts of suicide. I spent a fair amount of time and energy battling those thoughts and feelings. I remember driving along a river and thinking that all I would have to do is turn my steering wheel to the right and it would be all over. It wasn't that I really wanted to drown. It was more that I didn't feel alive, that so much of me was already dead.

I couldn't do the things I used to do. One day, I put on three pairs of pants, because I couldn't remember that I already had pants on. I accidentally created pepper spray by trying to cook and forgetting about a pan on the stove. Worse still, no one could tell me if I'd ever get any better, or if I'd ever feel things again.

My emotions were somehow locked away from me. I could observe feelings, but I couldn't feel them. The best way I can describe it is to say it was like living in a tube, with everything else outside and with me cut off.

Once again nature came to my rescue. Trees kept showing me their resilience and adaptability. They kept pointing my way forward, reminding me that sometimes a catastrophe is just a new beginning. I kept taking pictures of them, absorbing their message.

Solitude provides, or maybe insists on, an opportunity to view my own thoughts. I drove through beautiful scenery, sometimes becoming aware of how unaware I had been, becoming angry at the unawareness and going through that cycle over and over. As I watched my internal drama, I began to consider the drama

elsewhere in my life, in my relationships. These thoughts led me
to take a written inventory of where there were problems, and to
write down what needed to change in order to heal that. I called
everyone on the list to set new boundaries that would allow me
to offer love to them and to myself.

The goal of my journey was to make it to the Blood Reserve in
Alberta for ceremony. I had participated for years and wanted
to continue, but memories of who I had been sparked the fear
again. Would the leaders accept me as I was? Would I? How
could I serve in this new form that I believed to be broken?
I worried about these things as I neared my destination.

My last visit before I arrived was with Bill and his partner, Traci.
I knew them well and they welcomed Hunter and me in as family. They went out of their way to care for me, to share with me,
to offer me everything I needed to heal. My time there is one of
the most cherished memories of my journey.

As I left that haven of love and acceptance, I began to worry
about serving at ceremony again. I wondered if my contribu-
tions would be worthy, but what I really wondered was if I were
still worthy, if I still had value in this community that had been
so important to me. During those few days, I spent one night
in a grocery store parking lot in a small town. I remember that
I slept deeply. In the morning, Hunter and I were on our walk
when we ran into the most unlikely person to be in such a
setting, a woman who was a yoga practitioner and therapist, far
away from where you'd be likely to find any such things in this
little town of about 250 people. We chatted a bit, and she asked
how I was doing. I remember thinking it was an odd question.
Then it occurred to me, *"Maybe, just maybe, she asked because
she really wants to know."* I was so taken aback by this idea that
the conversation has stayed with me, and I still think about it

from time to time. I'm sure she has no idea that she made an important contribution to my recovery process.

Finally, I arrived. I set up camp, continuing to be anxious about how the leaders would respond to the new Wayne. Of course my worries, though quite real, had been groundless. I was welcomed with open arms and allowed to participate at a level that would allow for self-care. My leaders helped me set boundaries, a lesson that I continued to work on in all aspects of my life.

My journey toward home after ceremony was much the same. The lessons of a world full of love and kindness continued to appear wherever I looked. I spent time with friends and I made TBI mistakes. Sometimes they made me angry or afraid, but more and more often, I was able to laugh at myself with love and acceptance.

I will end with one last snippet of experience. I was camped at Salmon La Sac, a place I had not even intended to visit. It was my last stop before returning home. I had a beautiful camp site and spent the evening looking up at the stars, contemplating what I had learned on my journey. When I woke up in the morning, there were low clouds with mountain tops above them, towering over me. My experiences solidified in a new way as I opened even further. Maybe my TBI allowed me to see my surroundings with new eyes. Everything looked surreal, as if I were in a fantastical, magical world. Then, it all fell into place, like the tumblers as the key opens a lock. I realized that that magical world isn't a fantasy; it is the deep truth of the place I have always lived.

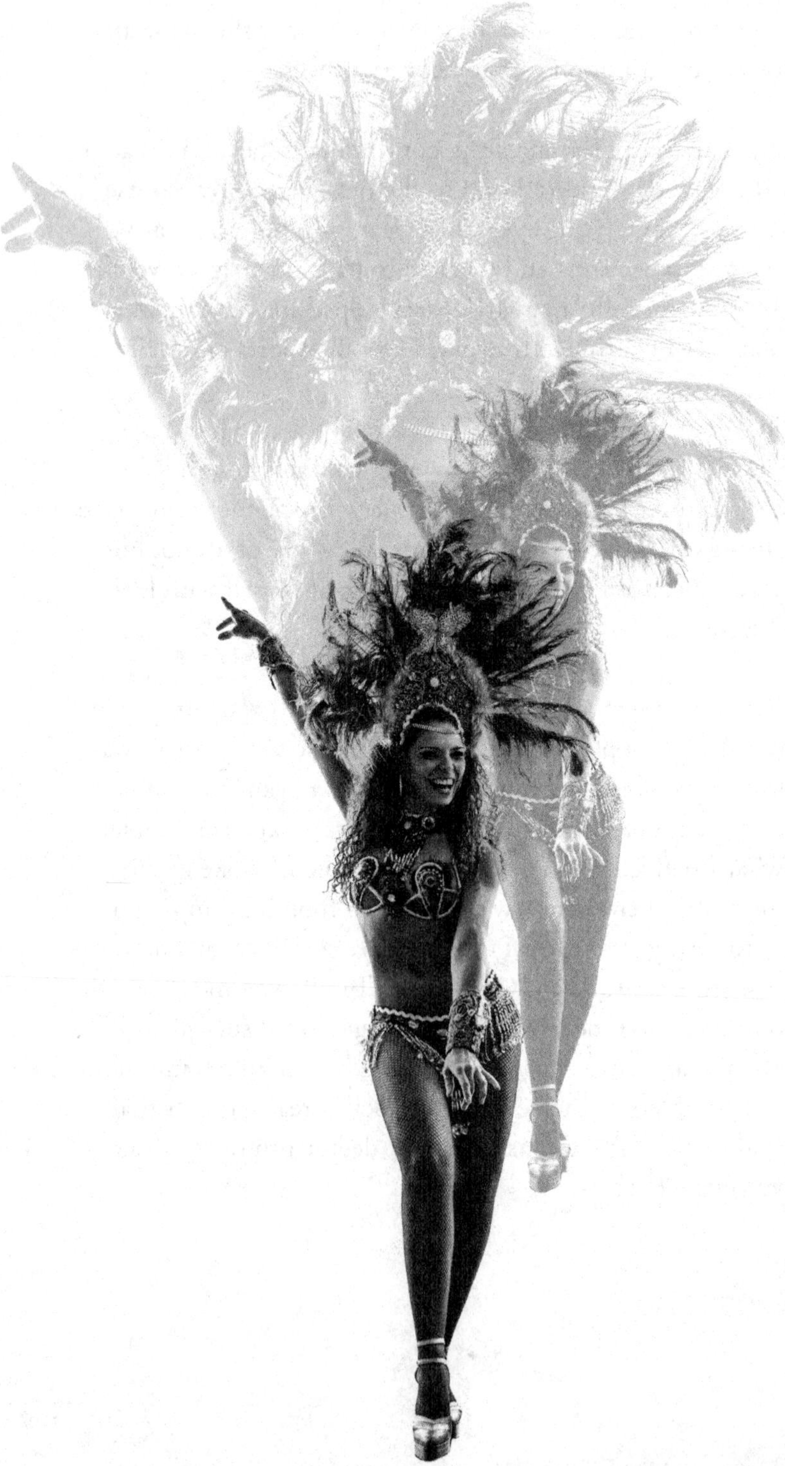

Chapter Seventeen

A FEW FINAL WORDS...

And so there you have it... sixteen amazing people sharing their own stories of Dancing in the unknown. Now it's your turn! How will you dance?

The trick to dancing is to just start moving, to close your eyes and feel your heart beat, reach out your arms and let your hips sway. It doesn't matter what you look like, it doesn't matter if you trip and fall, you will look both insane and clumsy, mostly to those still stuck along the wall. Move out into the middle of the dance floor and let go...

My beloved often says to me, as he watches my foot tap and my shoulders move, yearning to break out into dance...

"Don't worry, I hate to ruin the ending for you, but it's all going to be OK, so just dance baby, dance"
        –BRIAN WALSH
(Yes others have said it, but that's how he says it to me)

XO Betsy Chasse.

AND FOR FUN, SOME OTHER GREAT QUOTES ABOUT DANCING TO INSPIRE YOU;

"And those who were seen dancing were thought to be insane by those who could not hear the music."
    —Friedrich Nietzsche

"Dance, when you're broken open. Dance, if you've torn the bandage off. Dance in the middle of the fighting. Dance in your blood. Dance when you're perfectly free."
    —Jalaluddin Rumi

"We should consider every day lost on which we have not danced at least once."
    —Friedrich Nietzsche

"Dance is the hidden language of the soul"
    —Martha Graham

"Life is the dancer and you are the dance."
    —Eckhart Tolle, A New Earth:
    Awakening to Your Life's Purpose

"The only way to make sense out of change is to plunge into it, move with it, and join the dance."
    —Alan W. Watts

You can share your story too! Join our Facebook Group "Dancing In The Unknown". Share your story, meet the authors of this book, connect, inspire and be inspired.

CPSIA information can be obtained
at www.ICGtesting.com
Printed in the USA
FSOW04n1151260917
39199FS